Praise for

Can
We Do
That?

Here is a different book! While honoring Christian marriage and insisting on adherence to biblical principles, this Christian pastor and medical doctor swings wide open some reluctant old doors. Honest sexual questions are asked aloud and answered straightforwardly. Are you married or about to be married, committed to Jesus Christ, want all the joy and intimacy God has designed for his children–but you have lots of delicate questions? Then start reading these pages!

—Dr. Barry Callen, Distinguished Professor Emeritus of Christian Studies, Anderson University; Editor of the Wesleyan Theological Journal and Anderson University Press

If you have ever thought about it, but were afraid to ask, read on. *Can We Do That* will answer questions and provide scripture as basis for thought. I applaud the courageous approach this pastor has taken when confronting sensitive topics regarding Christian sexual behavior. Far too often the church has been reticent when addressing controversial subject matter. Christians have been reluctant to share their questions and desires for fear of rejection or condemnation. Rev. Dr. McNeese confronts many of these issues, answers the tough questions, and lends opportunity for continued dialogue.

—Rev. Arnetta Bailey, Executive Director, Women of the Church of God, Anderson, IN

I liked this manuscript … an excellent writer. The material is frank and compelling … Thank you so much for writing this work.

—Al Weir, M.D., VP for Campus and Community Membership, Christian Medical & Dental Associations, Bristol, TN

Can we do that? What a title for a book, I thought. However, the sorry, confused state of too many Christian marriages screams for this book. Dr. McNeese does a thorough job of examining many issues and questions that unfortunately go unaddressed, even in premarital sessions. Whether you totally agree or not with all of the author's findings, *Can We Do That* should be a part of the personal library of every married couple.

—Jerald January, Sr., Senior Pastor, Vernon Park Church of God, Chicago, IL

Noteworthy for reading...a subject matter that is still private and sensitive with a wide spectrum of dispositional beliefs...There will probably never be unanimous agreement concerning sexual preferences in a Christian marriage...however, the author has put forth vital information for authentic discussions and considerations in the life of the Christian couple.

—Bartholomew M. Riggins, M.Div.,
Senior Pastor Queensborough Church of God,
Shreveport, LA

Very well done...a help in the marital enrichment arsenal...Rev.Robinson-McNeese M.D. in *Can We Do That* provides a much needed foundational basis for a healthy sexual life in a Christian context. He takes a transparent look at an often closed topic that is informative, challenging and liberating.

—Elder Derrol Dawkins, M.D.,
Senior Pastor, Northside Church of God,
Birmingham, AL

Can We Do That?

We love you, Diane.
Follow Him!

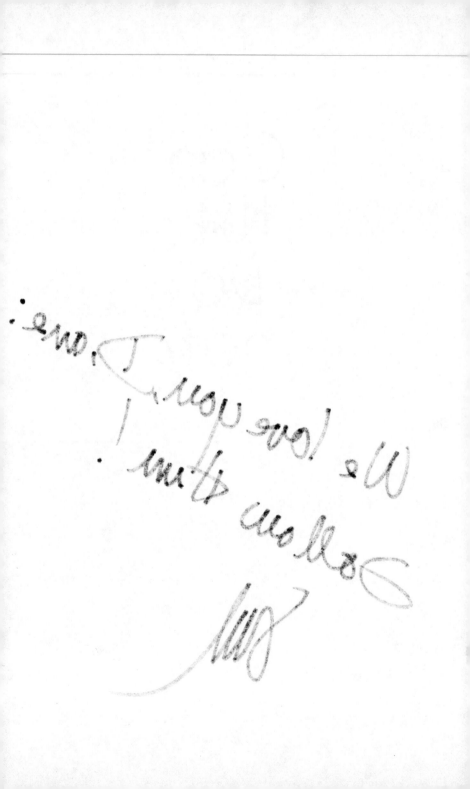

Can We Do That?

W.G. Robinson-McNeese M.D.

TATE PUBLISHING & *Enterprises*

Published by Tate Publishing & Enterprises, LLC
127 E. Trade Center Terrace | Mustang, Oklahoma 73064 USA
1.888.361.9473 | www.tatepublishing.com

Tate Publishing is committed to excellence in the publishing industry. The company reflects the philosophy established by the founders, based on Psalm 68:11,
"The Lord gave the word and great was the company of those who published it."

Book design copyright © 2009 by Tate Publishing, LLC. All rights reserved.
Cover design by Tyler Evans
Interior design by Blake Brasor

Published in the United States of America

ISBN: 978-1-61566-285-2
1. Health & Fitness, Sexuality
2. Religion, Sexuality & Gender Studies
09.10.28

Dedication

This book is dedicated to my wife—who is my confidante, my cheering section, and my love; to my mother—whose voice I still hear in quiet times and who gave me a strong appreciation for the power of the written and spoken word; to the other women in my family—who have modeled faith, fidelity, and femininity for me over the years; to my children, siblings, and friends—who reviewed this material during its evolution and gave critical feedback; and to my medical school co-worker—who asked the provocative question, "Dr. McNeese, why don't you stop talking about doing it and just write the book?"

Table
of
Contents

Foreword

by LaVern A. McNeese

It is an honor to write the foreword for my husband's book. The first draft of his manuscript was eye-opening, especially for me, whom my husband teasingly refers to as a prude. His frank discussion of such topics as cunnilingus, fellatio, masturbation and orgasm caused me to fidget and to feel a bit uncomfortable. In fact, because of my lack of formal exposure to sexual information, some of the terms I knew very little about, and others I did not recognize at all.

Discussions of sexual matters were taboo during my adolescent years and even beyond. The adults around me didn't dare touch on such sensitive, intimate subjects except jokingly or in whispers, as if to do so was sinful and dirty. No parent, teacher or minister I knew ever gave any detail about this special sexual gift given by God. It's no wonder so many of us Christian women are confused and uptight about our sexual thoughts, actions, and especially inactions. Christian men seem misguided as well.

After reading this book, I now know that there's nothing inherently immoral about sex and sex acts performed within a married relationship. I agree with my husband who writes "God gave us a sex drive to assure propagation, but also to give us pleasure" and that God wants us "to confine sexual exploits to marriage." Furthermore, he writes that most sexual behaviors performed by a married couple are acceptable in God's eye. All of this information (revelation to me) helps put my mind at ease.

While I no longer feel confused about appropriate sexual thoughts and behavior, I am still working to free myself of some sexual inhibitions–learning to relax and freely enjoy this beautiful gift given us by our Creator. This book has helped me greatly, and I truly believe it will be just as helpful to you if you read it with an open mind and open heart.

I am grateful to God for working through Wesley to provide a book that encourages sexual freedom and promotes sexual happiness among Christian couples. He's quite a man, and this is quite a book!

Introduction

During one of many amorous encounters shared with my wife of thirty-two years, while positioning myself for a maneuver that I thought surely would result in mutual sexual satisfaction and pleasure, she stopped me and asked, "Can we do that?" Her question revolved around whether my romantic plans were biblically based and consistent with what Christian couples were permitted to do in bed. Or, in other words, was God going to get us for what I was about to do?

While my timing was near perfect, hers was not, and due to the urgency of the moment and my unwilling-ness to give a detailed explanation just then, I answered, "Yes, sweetheart, yes, we can do this, and I'm about to get to it right now!"

This book was written (during more settled times) to finally answer her question (with some elaboration). I have addressed a few other related topics and thorny issues and am determined to share these thoughts about sexuality with my Christian sisters and brothers.

The manuscript is written with a decidedly Christian perspective. It is an exposition of sexual thought and behavior, and not a physiology text or how-to sex manual; no medical advice is being given or diagnoses made.

The writing represents one pastor's opinions about several subjects and is aimed mainly at Christian, married couples. Those who someday hope to be married will also benefit from reading these pages. A number of familiar sexual topics are commented upon using biblical reference, where possible, for guidance.

It is my prayer that people will read and use this book widely in workshops and didactic sessions, but especially in marital and premarital discussions to stimulate thought and conversation (to that end, discussion questions follow most chapters). It is hoped that these words will lead you to a better understanding of Christian sexuality, as it should be practiced in this present world.

Sexual
Thoughts

Is Sex
a Gift
from God?

One of the most beautiful gifts given by God to humanity is sexual nature. That nature, at its essence, is neither dirty nor destructive. It is, however, powerful and pervasive—an integral part of our human personality. God gave us a sex drive to assure propagation, but also to give us pleasure—physically and psychologically binding us to one another in a way no other human compulsion can.

Originally, this sexual gift was to be used and enjoyed without inhibitions by the first couple, but they sinned by disobeying God's instructions and following their own minds, thereby breaking the spiritual bond with God. When this sin spiritually separated humankind from God, the resulting relationship—creation to Creator—was strained and very different from the original design. The human sexual relationship also was changed by this transgression.

God, because he loves us, put together a plan of redemption for humanity: grace. Grace is unmerited love and forgiveness available to all—forgiveness for our sin. God gave his Son, Jesus Christ, as a sacrifice that paid our sin debt. Christ's death on the cross was a redemptive act that restored the spiritual connection between God and the human race, bringing back full fellowship.

Christ died in our stead, and his substitutionary death opened up a plan of restoration for all who would accept it: "Herein is love, not that we loved God, but that he loved us, and sent his Son to be the propitiation for our sins"(1 John 4:10). An offshoot of that plan is a set of prescribed actions that are indicative of those who have accepted Jesus Christ as their Savior and who choose to walk in his ways. These actions are both the goals and the guidelines for our daily living. These goals and guidelines are contained in what we now call the Bible. Adhering to these rules does not assure our salvation. Our salvation is assured by God's grace (grace being his unmerited gift to humankind). But, once saved, we try to follow the rules with all our hearts.

Christians are called upon to act in ways that seem peculiar to the world. Titus 2:14 teaches about the salvation plan, explaining that Jesus "gave himself for us, that he might redeem us from all iniquity and purify unto himself a peculiar people, zealous of good works." These good works that come from Christians and their peculiar ways of behaving have many dimensions, including very specific constraints placed on the expression of our sexual natures.

Although our sexual identities are on the one hand strong and simple, they are at other times challenging and complex. The challenge to harness our sexual urges

W.G. Robinson-McNeese, M.D.

is just as great for Christians as it is for the unsaved, but Christians are expected by God to align their sexual practices with the teachings of the Bible.

One cannot be unsaved and/or unwilling to follow God's rules for living but expect their marriages and sex lives to work well. The holy estate of marriage was meant to be carried out by holy people. It is because our society has abandoned the sacred principles that from the beginning characterized God's marriage plan that marriages, over the years, have increasingly become less stable, less palatable and ended in divorce.

Marital relationships are a challenge, even for Christians, but God gave principles to help Christian couples relate to one another and to fully experience the spiritual bond that sexuality and sharing life's experiences are intended to produce. Our Creator knew that the human sex drive unchecked would contaminate, complicate, and curse the lives of people here on earth. Therefore, Christ believers were told generally to confine sexual exploits to marriage and the marriage bed. God knew that his gift, unrestrained by a loving and gentle Christian ethic, would wreak havoc in this world. The havoc takes the form of sexual depravity and addiction, criminality, pornography, promiscuity, and sexually transmitted infections (to name but a few).

Do you remember the myth of "Pandora's Jar"? In it, a warning ignored leads to the spread of evil throughout the world. God's warning is far more preeminent and real than this myth. He cautions us that the sexual gift is a marvelous one, but to not open its wonders until circumstances are right and proper—marriage. Much of this world has ignored God's directions regarding sex and liberally engages in its myriad practices with little consideration of God's plan or of proper timing. As a result, a perverse sexual character has spread throughout the world.

Where there was supposed to be purity, we now have immorality. Where sex was meant to foster spiritual closeness, we have developed customs that are loose, crass, and dismissive. Where sex was meant to be a private, sacred experience between a man and a woman, it is now publicly secular. Multiple promiscuous sexual liaisons are the order of the day, and society hardly even blinks at such decadence.

This book is a call to Christians to return to the plan established by God for expressing our sexual personality; and a major part of that plan is marriage. Marriage is a sanctified union, a chosen state of living that is authorized and blessed by God. It was initiated by the Creator through the first couple, and was further clarified when in Genesis 2:24 it was declared, "Therefore shall a man leave his father and his mother, and shall cleave unto his wife: and they shall be one flesh." God created a condition where a man and a woman were positioned to complement, support, and sustain one another.

Over the ages, however, matrimony has been ransacked and hijacked by various worldly factions, and its character changed from what God intended. Unbridled eroticism has become the order of the day. A spill over effect is that marriage is being redefined, and much of the luster of the *holy estate* is being worn away. Many in contemporary society choose not to marry at all, but rather form sexual partnerships of various description and duration. Nonetheless, Christians are herein encouraged to reclaim marriage and make that relationship what God intended.

One of the strongest forces for intimate, male-female relationships is sexual attraction. Sex, from the beginning, was designed to be a cementing force for such associations, and it very effectively accomplishes that linkage in most cases (sex for hire and abusive sex are glaring exclusions); so much so that this bonding occurs whether a couple is Christian or not. The inevitable binding force of reciprocated sexual contact explains why most couples, regardless of beliefs, become strongly tied to one another following sexual intercourse, and why their unions are so addictive and difficult to terminate. In unmarried situations, the bond is genuine, but the relationship flies in the face of biblical teaching.

The first man declared about the first woman, "This is now bone of my bones, and flesh of my flesh" (Genesis 2:23). These words foreshadowed the physical coming together that would occur between the two sexes, over and over again. Men and women unite on so many levels, and the sexual level is but one, albeit a very powerful one. Sexual commingling is predestined for humans; as in a sense, we seek to reconnect with ourselves. God simply wants us to connect in certain ways and under certain circumstances.

In this primer, several topics are commented upon and opinions given about how God would like us to deal with these erotic circumstances.

What Does the Bible Tell Us about Sex?

Christians are often closed and puritanical in their approach to sexuality. Many church people are sexually inhibited, and those inhibitions can make for less-than-satisfying sexual relationships. These inhibitions are frequently the result of customs and practices passed down from generation to generation, with little examination and comparison to scriptural direction. Many Christians were raised on the rigid "that's just the way it should be done" principle of sexual behavior, handed down by parents with little thought given to answering questions about what is to be done sexually, or how, why, and when it is to be done.

Since sexuality is infrequently preached from church pulpits and not often taught during Bible studies, except to warn or condemn, large numbers of Christian believers are confused about what is appropriate sexual thought and behavior. Workshops and classes on sexual topics are mainly confined to special retreats and other closed gatherings, so that our handling of the subject leads parishioners—especially young ones—to believe there is a far-reaching taboo and closely guarded secret associated with sex and all things sexual. This reluctance by the church to regularly discuss erotic topics has led to widespread ignorance among its followers about acceptable sexual practices. For many, this ignorance leads to repressed, guilt-ridden expressions of passion, even in their bedrooms.

At the seat of this repression is an antiquated belief that sex is meant for propagation only—"be fruitful, multiply and replenish the earth" (Genesis 1:28)—and any enjoyment derived from the sexual encounter is somehow inappropriate and sinful. Such belief in the procreative-only nature of sex was reinforced by the effects of seventeenth century Puritanism on the Christian culture and its emphasis on deprivation and self-denial. Consequently, generations of Christians have come of age restrained by the belief that sex is something you do, but not something you enjoy or talk about—at least not openly.

Such an interpretation of Genesis 1:28 puts more emphasis on what that scripture explicitly directs, "multiply and replenish," than on the sexual messages implied and described in this verse and others throughout the Bible. For example, a command such as this one is very straightforward, but it does not explicitly answer the questions: What should be the nature of the multiplication, and when are we to do it? For answers to these and other related questions, one must look at other scriptures. And, again, in the absence of a specific directive, make judgments about what those scriptures infer or imply.

Individuals do not multiply and replenish in a vacuum. Sexual forces must be in play to bring men and women physically together so that multiplication can take place. Similar sexual forces must work to keep couples together to form satisfying, monogamous relationships. The Bible gives numerous examples of sexual relationships played out before God and describes for us the things about those relationships that are good and desirable, as well as bad and forbidden. Because the subject of Christian sexuality largely has been kept under wraps, we've learned to wrap it in our own idiosyncratic rituals and only periodically get public, Christian instruction about what the Bible has to say on the topic.

Most of the sexual information in the Bible is meant to sanction, strengthen, and encourage heterosexual marriage. Amorous, biblical references are for wedded, Christian couples (women and men) and not for instruction in premarital or extramarital relationships. While the Bible is not at its basis a sexual primer, the holy Scriptures give ample evidence of the sexual mores of Old and New Testament believers. Where the Bible does not speak to sexual matters directly, it leaves clues to guide our behavior. We only need plumb the numerous biblical stories to come away with a contemporary set of directions about what to do and what not to do sexually.

Biblical principles can and should be applied to sexual activities of today, because the Bible is a timeless document. God has not changed his mind about how he wants Christians to behave in their erotic lives. Truly, as far as sexual practices go, there is "no new thing under the sun" (Ecclesiastes 1:9), just new devices and venues. The sexual practices of the Old and New Testament, when critically evaluated and interpreted, give ample guidance about how we should behave today. As you read this book, you should check the Scriptures cited, and related ones, using your own Bible, its translations, and commentaries for reference.

Adult sexual habits and beliefs are largely the result of lessons learned during childhood. Regrettably, many of us are never formally taught about sex either as children or adults. The birds and the bees is a topic that is glossed over by many parents. Primary and high school-directed sex-education classes are superficial at best, limited by teacher knowledge and motivation, curriculum, schedules, as well as controversy over what should be taught in these classes and whether such classes should be taught at all. As a result, in the main, we are obliged to learn our sexual behaviors and attitudes from experimentation, exploitation, best-friend secrets, the Internet, and other media.

In so many instances, the sexual lessons learned during formative years are handed down with little explanation or rationale, or they are twisted and poisoned by miscreants with no moral compass. Acceptable sexual behavior is even more perplexing for Christians who often view their sensuous information through a worldly prism, because religious leaders are much too silent on the issues or deliver stern *thou shalt not* messages on intimacies that give little detail and even less direction.

These following chapters will answer the question posed in the title of this book and tie those responses to many specific sexual practices. The most direct reply

I can give now to the question, "Can we do that?" is this: "Yes, yes, you probably can!" The word *probably* is used here only because later in this book you will be given specific instances where you should not do a particular thing. At any rate, you are encouraged to follow my words from the introduction, and "get at it right now." Enjoy your sexual lives while you are still ready and able.

In the Bible there is no one scripture that directs Christians to not have sex before marriage. There is, however, a scripture that strongly implies this prohibition—1 Corinthians 7:2. This scripture encourages, "Nevertheless, to avoid fornication, let every man have his own wife, and let every woman have her own husband." In the latter part of the chapter preceding this one, the Apostle Paul has given instructions that Christians should flee fornication because it is a sin against the body (and the spirit). He goes on to talk in chapter seven, verse two, about what Christians should do to avoid the sin of fornication. If fornication (sex outside marriage) was not a sin, then chapter seven, verse two, would be illogical and nonsensical.

The Bible instructs that coitus—copulation— should only take place within the marriage relationship; it warns against four types of unacceptable sexual behavior. The categories are:

> *Extramarital*—sex with anyone other than your spouse (includes premarital and group sex)
> *Group*—sex involving three or more people (sometimes referred to as an orgy)
> *Anal*—sex involving copulation through the anus
> *Menstrual*—copulation at the time of menses

Extramarital, premarital, and group sex are described in the Bible as forms of *fornication—consenting sex involving someone unmarried.* Anal sex (sodomy) and sex during menses will be discussed more fully in later chapters.

Group sex involves a husband and wife joining with one or more other people for sexual intercourse; this is debauchery and unacceptable behavior for a Christian. While the Bible does not specifically direct, "Don't have group sex," it certainly indicates that monogamy is preferred. Recall again Genesis 2:24. This scripture points out that a man shall "leave his father and his mother, and cleave unto his wife: and they shall be one flesh." This passage instructs Christians to cling to one another and to join flesh together sufficient enough for them to become one spiritual unit. This declaration leaves no room for other sexual partners beyond the unit. The sex act is meant to be interplay between two individuals—a man and a woman. While the act may have many variations and be carried out on many stages, it was designed for two heterosexual characters only.

Orgies are unbridled, licentious parties that feature heavy sexual involvement. There is scripture that purports to deal specifically with orgiastic behavior: Galatians 5:21—"Envyings, murders, drunkenness, revellings, and such like: of the which I tell you before, as I have also told you in time past, that they which do such things shall not inherit the kingdom of God."

"Revellings" are believed by many theologians to mean sexual behavior that includes riotous partying and orgies. The International Standard Bible Encyclopedia defines reveling as, "orgiastic heathen worship; classed with fornication, uncleanness and lasciviousness; excessive and boisterous, lustful indulgence."

An incident recounted in Numbers 25:1–3 would qualify as one of reveling.

> And Israel abode in Shittim, and the people began to commit whoredom with the daughters of Moab. And they called the people unto the sacrifices of their gods: and the people did eat, and bowed down to their gods. And Israel joined himself unto Baalpeor: and the anger of the Lord was kindled against Israel.

When the men of Israel began to have sex with the Moabitesses of Shittim, their behavior was orgiastic, since worship of the idol Baalpeor was characterized by licentious sexual doings that included unclean rites, public prostitution, and bestiality. God's reaction to that behavior and his subsequent penalty of death for the men, who participated in those salacious acts, is without question because they participated in the worship of another god, but also because of the nature of the participation. God abhors revellings and lasciviousness, and lists these acts among several other "works of the flesh" mentioned in Galatians 5:19–21.

Most other sexual behaviors are fair game and open to all able-bodied Christians if they meet the condition—marriage (defined as a legally solemnized union between a man and a woman). You should relax and enjoy this part of your physical and spiritual make up. Great enjoyment and pleasure can be found in your spouse and your spouse alone. God will bless your marriage union in many ways, including sexually, if you dedicate your life to finding and doing the things that are pleasing in his sight.

Is the Sky the Limit?

Hebrews 13:4 declares, "Marriage is honourable in all, and the bed undefiled." This scripture is the underlying premise of this book, and most conclusions reached in this writing relate back to the assertion: There is very little that can be done sexually between a husband and wife that is forbidden. While individual preferences, tastes, and teachings will heavily influence one's sexual practices, the Bible speaks against but a few broad categories of sexual conduct. Various Bible commentators have spoken to the meaning of this phrase from Hebrews chapter thirteen.

Adam Clarke believes the marriage state is to "be highly esteemed as one of God's own instituting," and interprets the bed undefiled to mean: "every man cleaving to his own wife, and every wife cleaving to her own husband." [Adam Clarke's Commentary on the New Testament, Quick Verse 2008 12.0.2 (Dec 27 2007 19:33:43]

Barnes emphasizes that "honor is to be shown to the marriage relation. It is not to be undervalued by the pretence of superior purity of a state of celibacy." The bed undefiled is interpreted to mean: there should be "fidelity to the marriage vow." [Barnes' Notes on the New Testament, Quick Verse 2008 12.0.2 (Dec 27 2007 19:33:43]

Matthew Henry believes that marriage should be "esteemed by all." This commentator says of the undefiled bed: It is when "persons come together pure and chaste, and preserve the marriage bed undefiled, not only from unlawful but inordinate affections ... a dreadful but just censure of impurity and lewdness: whoremongers and adulterers God will judge." [Matthew Henry's Commentary on the New Testament, Quick Verse 2008 12.0.2 (Dec 27 2007 19:33:43]

The IVP Background Bible Commentary teaches that the word *bed* was an "idiom for intercourse ... male sexual immorality was rife in Greco-Roman society, which also accepted prostitution, pedophilia, homosexual intercourse, and sex with female slaves." [The IVP Bible Commentary: New Testament, Quick Verse 2008 12.0.2 (Dec 27 2007 19:33:43]

The Believer's Study Bible says that the phrase is a "refutation of asceticism ... a call to purity within marriage ... God is the author of sexuality. As long as the expression of intimacy exists exclusively between husband and wife, it is undefiled and honorable." [The Believer's Study Bible, Quick Verse 2008 12.0.2 (Dec 27 2007 19:33:43]

This book interprets the Hebrew chapter thirteen scriptural phrase most like the IVP and Believer's Bible commentaries. Many people will sight in on the phrase *in all* and assert that any and all sexual behaviors in marriage are acceptable and sanctioned by the Bible. To do so is to fall victim to the widespread practice of reading a scripture and settling on its meaning without examining its context, or other scriptures that deal with that and similar subject matter. In this particular scripture, the phrase *in all* speaks more to the acceptance of marriage than to its practices; the phrase is best interpreted to mean *among all*, or *esteemed by all*.

This scripture teaches that God sees marriage as an honorable and holy estate. It was established by him and is carried out with his approval. Marriage is the primary way God wants a man and a woman to relate to one another when they are in love—when they want to live together, and especially when they want to bear children. The phrase *bed undefiled*, used in concert with marriage, suggests there is very little a married couple can do together sexually that would desecrate the sanctity of their union or run them afoul of God's wishes.

Remember, however, the full body of scripture that deals with marriage and sexuality, must be taken into consideration when trying to understand God's wishes for us regarding sex in marriage. The full body of scripture that deals with this subject leads to the following interpretation of Hebrews 13:4: There are few taboos in the bedroom between man and wife, but sodomy is one. Sodomy is singled out here because the Bible indirectly, but forthrightly, condemns this practice. The King James Version of the Bible does not expressly mention the word sodomy (Sodom and Sodomite are mentioned, however).

Sodomy is "anal intercourse between two men or sexual relations between people and animals; any of various forms of sexual intercourse held to be unnatural or abnormal, especially anal intercourse or bestiality" (Dictionary.com). The practice of sodomy is historically tied to the biblical cities of Sodom and Gomorrah, because it is believed anal intercourse was a prevalent sexual activity in those localities. In Genesis nineteen, the story is told of two angels who came to visit Lot in the city of Sodom, and how these visitors were accosted by men of Sodom who wanted to have sex with the saintly guests: "And they called unto Lot, and said unto him, Where are the men which came in to thee this night? Bring them out unto us, that we may know them" (verse five).

Lot eventually offered his daughters to the men to divert their attention from the angels, but the men of the city rejected the women and instead pressed for sex with the male visitors. God eventually destroyed these two cities because of his disdain for their sinful lives and the sexual practices that were prevalent there. "Then the Lord rained upon Sodom and upon Gomorrah brimstone and the fire from the Lord out of heaven; and he overthrew those cities, and all the plain, and all the inhabitants of the cities, and that which grew upon the ground" (verses twenty-four and twenty-five).

Webster's dictionary's definition of *sodomy* is: "Anal or oral copulation (sexual intercourse; a joining together) with a member of the same or opposite sex; bestiality." Webster's definition confuses the issue for most individuals when it brings oral copulation into the matter. Typically, sodomy does not refer to oral copulation, but anal copulation only, especially men with men. It is assumed above that Webster's definition speaks of male-to-male oral copulation and not that of opposite sexes. Typically, when used in a religious context, sodomy describes homoerotic sexual acts, especially anal intercourse and, to a lesser extent, bestiality. So, while Hebrew 13:4 describes marriage as being "honourable in all," that really means in all except sodomy, bestiality, and the other forms of fornication mentioned earlier.

There is quick and easy agreement between most people against bestiality, so these writings won't dwell on that topic except to acknowledge that the practice exists and to condemn it outright as anti-Christian and psychologically suspect. A relevant scripture regarding bestiality is: "Neither shalt thou lie with any beast to defile thyself therewith: neither shall any woman stand before a beast to lie down thereto: it is confusion" (Leviticus 18:23).

Bestiality has been practiced over the ages and certainly existed in ancient biblical times. Ostensibly, bestiality is less prevalent today than in biblical times. Often during ancient forms of idol worship, women would offer themselves sexually to goats, dogs, and other male animals; men would copulate with various female animals. The Bible describes this practice as *confusion*, which is to say, it represents a form of sexual disorientation—an incomprehension and failure to acknowledge things that are godly.

This book breaks with Webster's sodomy definition where it includes oral copulation and will speak to that issue more in the cunnilingus and fellatio chapters. According to common understanding, modern day law, and religious usage, sodomy is anal intercourse with a member of the same or opposite sex. Anal intercourse, reportedly, is a mainstay of homosexual copulation. If this is true, then anal intercourse carried out by Christians is wrong on at least two levels. First of all, men should not have sexual intercourse with men; and secondarily, sexual intercourse should not be done through the anus (sodomy) because it is unnatural. "Thou shalt not lie with mankind, as with womankind: it is abomination" (Leviticus 18:22).

To be clearer, sexual intercourse should not be done through the anus of a woman or a man. The anal orifice and sphincter, while highly distensible, are anatomically designed for egress of materials and not ingress. Even the peristaltic (wave-like muscular contractions of a tubular structure) motion of the bowels above the orifice directs towards egress. And while the anus is most definitely an orifice, it was not intended by God for sexual intercourse, but for elimination of human waste products. These natural, physiologic realities give credence to scripture that describes sodomitic practices as being "against nature…the men, leaving the natural use of the woman, burned in their lust one toward another; men with men working that which is unseemly" (Romans 1:26–27).

For the record, sexual intercourse between two women also is not acceptable, Christian behavior; "women did change the natural use into that which is against nature" (Romans 1:26). This scripture further describes such homosexual practices between women as being contrary to the natural use of a woman's body (male-female copulation) and as *vile affections*.

So, sodomy and bestiality notwithstanding, married Christian couples (remember the definition of matrimony mentioned above) are free to do practically anything that gives them mutual sexual satisfaction and pleasure. The sky is the limit—almost; *almost*, because our sexual appetites can sometimes take us into ill-informed, ill-conceived, unhealthy, and illegal arenas. Later chapters deal with a few other things that will keep the marriage *bed undefiled*.

Summary Points:

- Sodomy and bestiality should not be part of Christian, married sexual relations; stay away from these practices altogether.
- Heterosexual oral sex is not a form of sodomy.
- Sodomy not only includes anal sex between two males, but also between a male and a female.
- Sex in marriage should be limited only by your imaginations, and by prohibitions against all forms of fornication.

Discussion Questions:

- The men of Sodom spoke of wanting to *know* the two angels who visited Lot. In this scripture (Genesis 19:5) what is meant by that word, *know*?
- Fornication can be both *homoerotic* and *heteroerotic* in nature; is one form worse than the other?

- Is bestiality a sin of the past; what proof do you have for your answer to this question?
- Do biblical teachings grant married couples permission to do all things sexual? Explain your answer.
- What is the biblical remedy for sexual sin?

W.G. Robinson-McNeese, M.D.

Whose Body
Is It
Anyway?

A seasoned marriage counselor once said, "Any couple married longer than a year who tells you they never fight or disagree is either lying to you or lying to them-selves." Likewise, couples who have been married for any significant length of time usually have disagreed about some sexual matter. In an ideal world, wives and husbands rarely, if ever, disagree, and they have sexual appetites that are totally in sync and easily satisfied. But ours is not an ideal world. Anyone who has been married longer than the honeymoon period knows that marital bliss is not defined by agreement on all sub-jects or the synchronicity of our sexual time clocks. If it were, then no married couples could claim happiness with their relationships. Happy marriages are identified more by how disagreement is handled, rather than by agreement on all subjects.

Most married couples will occasionally disagree about sex—what kind of sex, when to have sex, where to have sex, how much sex to have, etc. Christians usually do not discuss these critical, sexual relationship matters in great detail prior to marriage, but they should.

In addition to premarital conversations about finances, living spaces, and a plethora of other issues, we should engage in conversations about sexual preferences and expectations. If more such discussions were held before marriage, there would be less sexual frustration and disappointment once couples have come together. These types of discussions are not for the casual relationship, however; but rather for committed relationships that are pointing toward and on the cusp of marriage. Such discussions might best be carried out in the presence of your spiritual advisor and/or marriage counselor. In truth, most detailed, intimate discussions of sexual preferences are a definite prelude to sexual intercourse; so, be warned, when you talk this (sexual) talk, usually walking the walk is not far behind.

That being said, husbands and wives owe themselves to one another. The Bible introduces this principle in 1 Corinthians 7:3–4: "Let the husband render unto the wife due benevolence: and likewise also the wife unto the husband. The wife hath not power of her own body, but the husband: and likewise also the husband hath not power of his own body, but the wife."

Benevolence is a disposition or a desire to perform kindly deeds; a gift given out of generosity. Interestingly, in English history, benevolence was also the name given to forced contributions to the crown, mentioned here only to point out there should never be anything forced about today's Christian benevolence between husband and wife; that's oxymoronic.

There is little disagreement among theologians about the meaning of this word *benevolence* in the context of the Corinthians chapter seven scripture, especially when that scripture goes on to explain how married couples do not have power over their own bodies. This verse assuredly speaks about spouses being kind, gentle, and considerate to one another on all levels of their relationship, but most especially speaks to the idea that husbands should participate with their wives in sexual intercourse whenever their wives want it, and wives should do the same for husbands. Once you are married, your sexual apparatus is no longer just yours, but it is now to be shared with your spouse, abundantly, if your spouse so desires. So, whose body is it anyway? Well, it's yours, of course, but it is also your spouse's when they want it. This is not to suggest that spouses should demand sexual intercourse or force their partners; it is to suggest that partners should give sexual intercourse because it is a marital duty.

Following a marriage counseling session with a woman and her husband, the woman volunteered this summarization, "So, Pastor, you're saying that every time my husband gets hot, it's my job to put out the fire?" What a great question! She got the point of that particular session.

Sometimes your spouse's sexual fire will flare up for the strangest reason, at the most unexpected time, but it is still your job to "put out the fire." Both spouses owe this kindness to one another. Remember, sexual intercourse, does not always involve vaginal penetration; so you can be creative about how you quench the burning yearning. There are other ways to extinguish a raging sexual appetite besides coitus.

You won't always be able to satisfy your spouse's sexual craving the moment it occurs, but don't put off the job any longer than necessary. By the way, *job* is not such an unreasonable word to use in this context, because there will be times when giving your spouse sexual satisfaction will not be your number one priority. Even so, you must shift your priorities and take care of that marital task in a timely fashion. Just as you would dutifully perform the assignments related to your daily workplace employment, you should dutifully give your spouse this type of benevolence at home or in other appropriate places. Also, while giving your spouse sexual satisfaction, your goal should be to give what is wanted, when it is wanted and in portions big enough to satisfy.

It is not a good idea to repeatedly pepper your spouse with the question, "Was it good for you?" but you should be determined to satisfy your mate sexually, even if it means going a bit above and beyond where you want to go.

Prenuptial discussions of this topic are essential so potential spouses are not later surprised by the voraciousness of their partner's sexual appetite, or its near absence. Remember, our sexual proclivities are shaped by years of experiences and societal cues. It is no wonder some of us are tightly wrapped sexually and others of us as loose as a goose.

There are other precepts in 1 Corinthians chapter seven that are worth mentioning in this context. Verse one: "Now concerning the things whereof ye wrote unto me: It is good for a man not to touch a woman." The writer is saying here that if you are of a mind to spend your life celibate and to focus your strength on your relationship with the Lord and/or other matters, rather than a sexual relationship with someone of the opposite sex, then that's *good*. Concentrated, spiritual focus, and fervency, exclusive of sex, is a powerful discipline; not many have mastered such physical regulation. You should not feel ashamed of this leaning toward sexual abstinence or think yourself any less than someone else who chooses intimate man-woman relationships. But, do not be deceived. Celibacy is not a prerequisite for salvation or the Christian walk, nor is it evidence of it. If you're reading this book, you have likely gone past the point of not wanting to intimately touch or be touched by the opposite sex, so this scripture does not now apply to you, but is more a point of education.

Verse two: "Nevertheless, to avoid fornication, let every man have his own wife, and let every woman have her own husband." God's plan to manage the sexual urges that are ours and to multiply the human race is marriage—not premarital, or extramarital sex: "It is better to marry than to burn" (verse nine)—to burn in your lusts, to burn in damnation! The world has long since left this biblical principle behind. We live in a fornicating generation. Everybody's doing it, and doing it at younger and younger ages, without guilt or shame. Acts of fornication are pervasive in our media, literature and relationships. This promiscuity has caused damage to bodies, psyches, and affected every aspect of our society. The ultimate response from God to our sexual misconduct will be too hot for any to handle. Unequivocally, fornication is sin—one of the biggest and most wide-spread. Regardless of the stance taken by the world on this matter, we as Christians must stand against it in the name of the Lord, and in his strength. We must not back down; and if you plan to read on in this book, you will see that stance articulated again and again.

Verse five: "Defraud ye not one the other, except it be with consent for a time, that ye may give your-selves to fasting and prayer; and come together again, that Satan tempt you not for your incontinency." Don't cheat or be fraudulent with the *due benevolence* princi-ple. There will be psychological (bereavement, depres-sion, distraction, etc.) and physical (illness, injury, recu-peration, etc.) reasons to abstain from copulation espe-cially and other forms of sexual intercourse. Scripture teaches that sexual abstinence in married relationships should be done *with consent*. In other words, you and your spouse should discuss and agree upon the reasons to abstain. And you should agree that this backing away from sex will be *for a time* specified. A God-fearing and therefore reasonable spouse should understand these occasional interruptions, and should not give you too much grief about them.

There are few more laudable reasons than *fasting* and *prayer* to abstain from sex, but even then, spouses should agree on the plan. If God is calling you to that type devotion (temporarily), then ask God to help your spouse understand. While you may be in a fasting and praying mood, your spouse may not be. Plus, there is nothing about fasting and praying that absolutely requires abstinence from sex. The Bible suggests that to back away from sex without consent of your spouse is to set up one or the other of the partners to be tempted by sexual thoughts that wander outside the home.

The scripture that directs wives to "submit yourselves unto your husbands" (Ephesians 5:22), is not a scripture about sex alone (though many demanding husbands try to use it in that way). This scripture talks about submission on many levels of the relationship and is aimed mostly at establishing the man as the spiritual head of the marriage and therefore the family—again, God's plan. This oft-quoted scripture is preceded by one that instructs both couples to submit "one to another in the fear of God" (verse twenty-one). Men often gloss over this particular scripture because it seems to dilute their authority. There really is no dilution meant here, but rather a description of the most favorable atmosphere for submission to work—when both partners fear God.

A man's Bible-directed status in marriage and home is not a free ticket to be a kingly dictator, but rather an obligation to be a kindly director. The twenty-eighth and twenty-ninth verses of that same chapter remind men to "love their wives as their own bodies;" to nourish and cherish wives "even as the Lord the church."

Keep in mind that agreeing to have sex with your spouse does not necessarily equate to wanting to have sex with your spouse, or to actively initiating sexual contact. While the Bible is very clear and direct about our sexual duty to one another, most spouses would prefer a partner who truly desires them and not one who performs sexual favors out of a sense of obligation alone. You should not lie to your spouse at these times, but *duty sex*, when it occurs, should be performed as convincingly as possible, with great effort made to spare your partner's ego and feelings. Hopefully, this type sex will not happen in your relationship very often.

Finally, the principle of due benevolence is a sin-tight (exclusive of sin) system devised by the Lord. It is meant for committed Christian wives and husbands, and works only when both parties are closely following the relevant biblical directives. Whenever sinful attitude and behavior enter into this system, the arrangement is tainted and will not work as planned. Both spouses must have embraced God's due benevolence plan. So don't try bits and pieces of the plan and then complain when it isn't working. Don't fail to do your part but then expect your spouse to be exacting and faithful in doing his or her part. Give yourself fully to all that the Word speaks on the subject. Give yourselves freely and happily to one another and enjoy the sexual gift given so sweetly by the Lord. You are due this benevolence.

Summary Points:

- Discussions of sexual expectations are a must before engaged couples enter into marriage.
- Once married, your body is no longer just yours but belongs to your spouse as well.
- The biblical principle of *due benevolence* teaches (among other things) that your spouse is due sexual intercourse and sexual satisfaction from you; it is your duty.
- When you are led to abstain from sexual intercourse, you should prayerfully examine your reasons and then discuss them with

your spouse. The two of you should agree before you abstain.

Discussion Questions:

- Why is submitting to one another such a difficult principle for Christians to embrace?
- Does the Bible suggest that wives should be more submissive than husbands?
- Discuss *duty sex* from both vantage points and how you would want your spouse to handle such a circumstance.
- In what other areas of marriage is the principle of *due benevolence* applicable?
- When God calls you to *fasting and prayer*, do you think he informs your spouse at the same time?
- *Due benevolence* requires consenting and agreeing Christian spouses; why is that true?

Is Spousal Rape Possible?

Dictionaries define rape as the unlawful compelling of a woman through physical force or duress to have sexual intercourse. Rape, of course, can be carried out on a man as well, but the instances are relatively rare in regular society. Prison rape is commonplace and has devastating sequelae for its male and female victims, but discussion of these violent insults, carried out behind prison walls is beyond the scope of this book.

Rape, first and foremost, is an act of dominance, followed by grave sexual offense. Rape is at once immoral, illegal, and totally unchristian. In governmental records from two years ago, 95,000 rapes were reported to law enforcement agencies, and the numbers have increased in recent years. So many rapes go unreported by the victims. Three major reasons victims give for not reporting rapes are shame, fear, and the concern they will be blamed.

Most Christians would never think of themselves as rapists or having the mindset of a rapist. The forceful, sexual domination of another is something most

Christ-believers would consider foreign to the godly mentality or behavior code. Spousal rape is possible, however; also it is unacceptable behavior for any person, but especially those who count themselves as Christians.

Most spousal rapes go unreported. Many raped spouses feel they have no recourse and so suffer in silence. Some are so ashamed at the abuse they have suffered, they never tell anyone else about it. Others are confused about whether their spouse had the right to force sex on them.

Spouses who coerce their partners to have sex have gone far past decent conduct, let alone Christian conduct. Such a breach of another person's sexual dignity should not be tolerated by society's laws or the church polity. There is no justification for this violation of a person's physical and psychological space. Since most spousal rapes are carried out by husbands against wives, this book will primarily concentrate on that scenario. Reversal of this role, such that a woman forcibly dominates her husband in a sexual fashion, is just as unacceptable but is rare.

Many Christian men believe they have a right to have sex with their wives and can exercise this right whenever the mood hits them. Such men are fond of referring to the scripture that instructs wives to "submit yourselves unto your own husbands" (Ephesians 5:22), seeing this instruction as a directive to the wife to give sex on demand and also as a free pass to the husband to have sexual intercourse regardless of the wife's mood or circumstances. Such an interpretation of this scripture is incomplete, insensitive, and self-serving. This portion of scripture cannot rightly be lifted out of its full context and worn as a badge of male authority and sexual tyranny. Plus, this scripture speaks more to a spirit of overall submission than it does to the act of sexual submission.

In Ephesians five, the Apostle Paul gives a wealth of instructions on how the Christian life should be lived, using analogy liberally. Mis-interpreters of verse twenty-two from that chapter make their first mistake by not taking in the essence of the whole chapter, and most specifically by ignoring the message of verse twenty-one. In verse twenty-one, we are called to submit ourselves "one to another." This type spiritual submission trumps sexual longing every time; this verse suggests that wives and husbands should be trying to outdo one another in their unselfishness and giving, not the other way around. A spouse's well being should be of utmost importance to the other, and one should never commandeer the sexual discretion of the other by physically or mentally constraining them to submit to unwanted sexual intrusions.

Verse twenty-two from this chapter, therefore, is elaborative to verse twenty-one: "Wives submit yourselves unto your own husbands, as unto the Lord." A later scripture from the same chapter explains how this mutual submission should be accomplished: "Husbands, love your wives, even as Christ also loved the church, and gave himself for it" (verse 25).

Just as a loving, Christian woman has given her heart, body, and soul to Jesus for his service, so should she yield herself, in love, to her husband's position of authority. Just as Christ seeks and intercedes for the well-being of the church, a loving husband should put his wife's well-being on par with or above his own, and certainly should not wrest sex from his wife; to do so would be sexual larceny, not sexual love. A loving husband would give himself for his wife and would give up his personal wishes for hers. Such a husband would rather hurt himself than hurt his wife.

Paul uses the example of Christ being the head of the church to make the point that a wife should recognize the headship position the husband has in marriage, and respect *(reverence)* him in that role: "Nevertheless let every one of you in particular so love his wife even as himself; and the wife see that she reverence her husband" (verse thirty-three).

Likewise, the husband should love his wife as Christ loves the church, and make her welfare as important as his own. If these two conditions are not met, then no spouse can lift out a piece of the Scriptures' directives and use them as a spiritual cudgel to bully their spouse into giving sexual favors. If these two conditions are met, no spouse would rape or otherwise force themselves on their partner, because too much love is flowing between them to allow such a thing to happen. To rape your spouse would be inconsistent with an attitude of submission, reverence, and unselfish love. Spousal rape and other forms of sexual dominance are anathema to the holy marriage relationship.

Having said all this, if spouses are diligently practicing the principle of *due benevolence* and consistently communicating with one another, the specter of forcible sex should have less of an opportunity to slink into the married bed. If either spouse is *not in the mood*, then that spouse should let the other know this in a kind, considerate fashion. Go to great lengths to spare your partner's feelings and to assure them of your love and of your future receptiveness. The closing statement on this matter, nonetheless, is: Spousal rape is wrong and no legitimate excuse can ever be made for its occurrence.

Summary Points:

- Spousal rape does occur and it is unacceptable for a Christian to perpetrate such an insult and crime.
- *Due benevolence* does not mean one spouse can force sex upon another.

Discussion Questions:

- How many rapes were reported this past year?
- Do you think unreported rapes still outnumber reported ones? Explain your answer.
- If a spouse is raped, what is the place of church authority in the matter (if any)? What is the place of the police and legal authority (if any)?
- It has been said that true love and submission between a husband and wife are incompatible with spousal rape. Do you agree with this statement? Explain your answer.
- What should happen to one spouse who has raped the other?

What About Dating?

To *date* someone (socially speaking) is to set a special time and place to get together with that person, often to become better acquainted; usually some social exercise and venue is the backdrop—movie, restaurant, picnic, sports event, etc.—although dating can well take place at home. Where dating is concerned, emphasis here is placed on the word *special*. A couple should make special plans to go to a special place for a special experience together.

Married couples date for entertainment and enrichment of their relationships. Such couples have the advantage of a well-established connection, familiarity, and sexual intimacy, so their dates tend to flow more smoothly than for people who are unwed. For married couples, the mechanics of the date are rarely a problem; usually this group gets hung up on issues of occurrence and/or regularity.

Far too many individuals, once married, forget the enhancement value of sharing specially set aside time with their spouse. Married individuals should get away with one another on a date regularly. Doing so improves the relationship, if for no other reason than providing a change of scenery and activity. Plus, dating shows your spouse that you're still interested in being with them in a social setting, purely for the pleasure of their company. It is something of a cliché, but it's true: If you were interested in being out with your spouses before the marriage when you were trying to win their favor, you should be just as interested in dating them to keep their favor. To that end, married couples should date one another at least once per month.

Dating between two unmarried individuals is challenging for Christians, especially as the custom is practiced in the United States. And while unmarried couples on a date seek a similar enrichment as those who are married, the dynamics of dating for an unmarried couple are different and vary from person to person—culture to culture. Unmarried couples who date may hardly know one another and may, or may not, wish to be sexually intimate.

A century ago, those single couples going on a date were seeking to become better acquainted in preparation for marriage; so dating was a courtship ritual with a planned endpoint. Dating in past generations was frequently programmed and chaperoned to hopefully assure propriety. Christians and societal leaders from those past cultures realized how unwise it was to place two individuals with romantic leanings toward one another, and raging hormones, in close proximity and not expect sexual sparks or outright conflagration. The plan then was to permit dating but to forbid and prevent serious sexual interplay until marriage. We can argue how successful the plan was in those bygone years. Some cultures permitted no dating at all between partners prior to marriage. Many cultures still hold to this practice or some close approximation of it; these relationships tend to be a part of arranged marriages.

Today, most people date for the enjoyment of the encounter and the sexual contact that accompanies it. Thoughts about future marriage with the other party are superficially entertained, if at all. Often two people go on a date with different thoughts in mind about the purpose of the encounter and what is going to take place during it. These mixed objectives only add to the difficulty of dating, causing many people to dread the process, or at least feel a great deal of anxiety about it. Before going on a date, ask yourself why you are going and make sure the other person understands and accepts those parameters.

Modern dating comes in many forms—the classic one-on-one date, as described above (with or without chaperone), but also group dates, blind dates, and speed dates. Entrepreneurs have formed thriving businesses to assist daters, acting as matchmakers through personal consultations or through the Internet.

What makes dating tricky for Christians is that today's dating habits and expectations involve a great deal of sexual interplay—sex play that should be confined to marriage. Few scriptures speak directly about dating, although there is biblical documentation of different betrothals and their ultimate outcome. If dating had been transposed upon the ancient biblical world as we knew it, the expectation certainly would have been that individuals involved in courtship remain chaste and free from fornication. The chastity expectation is no less true for the modern Christian world, and there's the rub. Christians get carried away by the same sexual desires that come into the minds of non-Christians. However, the Bible calls on Christians to: "Abstain from all appearance of evil" (1 Thessalonians 5:22), and to "flee also youthful lusts" (2 Timothy 2:22).

Most people will not continue dating another person unless they have warm, and/or romantic feelings for that person—the object of their affections. Romantic feelings are the take off point for sexual expression. One need only spend a bit of time in the Songs of Solomon to learn how the physical appearance of someone you romantically care about—their smell, voice, or presence—can really set sexual urges in motion. These are legitimate urges, a part of God's sexual plan, but not meant to be exploited outside the marriage bed. For these reasons, if for no others, Christians should be of reasonable age, spiritual maturity, and sexual constraint before entering the dating arena.

Because of the way current customs define and describe dating, we set up Christians to fail by thrusting them into sexually intimate situations, but then expecting them to hold the line against certain forms of sexual involvement.

In this book, the faulty thinking about oral sex not being a form of sexual intercourse simply because there was no coitus involved, is explored. Contemporary daters have taken to engaging in all manner of sexual exploits, short of and including oral sex and copulation, to express their affection for one another; and in the process, they have defiled themselves—going against God's plan. Intimate sexual encounters should be confined to marriage. Christians cannot play with sexual fire, yet not expect to get sexually and spiritually burned.

If Christians are going to date—and evidence suggests they are—then they need to be careful in the process, take social precautions, and discuss expectations before doing so. Parents should discuss expectations with their children before those children begin a date. Both parents and child should know who, when, where, what, and other details about the date before it is allowed to take place. The persons dating should want to know similar particulars about the planned activity; and dating partners should have a fairly clear endpoint in mind for the date—something other than sex in some hidden place.

In today's world, dating can be a difficult proposition for anyone who is determined to keep his or her Christianity or virginity intact. There is no reason that Christians must discontinue dating. However, all dating Christians should be aware of the pitfalls mentioned above. Short of altogether restructuring our society's courtship rituals, we will have to bathe our dating practices in prayer, asking the Lord to guide, strengthen, and help us get through it all while preserving our sexual integrity.

The goal of dating—to enjoy one another's company and learn more about one another's personalities—is a laudable one. Laced heavily with prayer, this dating goal should help single Christians have a healthy social life and perhaps choose a good life partner.

Here's another statement for you to consider: Learn to be with you, then he may help you be with others—

anon. This statement emphasizes the need for all single Christians to properly arrange their priorities. Seek God first! Concentrate on your relationship with him; get that all polished up and acceptable in his sight. Fall in love with Jesus. And "all these things shall be added unto you" (Matthew 6:33). That promise may very well include a good date and a good partner for the future.

Summary Points:

- Christians should use dating for socialization, to learn about a person of interest, and for enjoyment, but not for ardent sexual interplay.
- Don't go on a date unless all parties involved know the parameters of the date and agree on the plan.
- Parents should not permit their children to date until the children have been taught the basics of male-female sexual interaction; also, have some assurance your child will not easily be carried away by *youthful lusts*.

Discussion Questions:

- How can you know if you and your intended are sexually compatible if you don't have sex before marriage? Don't you need to know?
- Surely heavy petting during dates is all right, isn't it?
- So, what's the point of dating if no sex is involved?
- What do you think about dating with chap-

erones in attendance? Should this be done? Explain.

- During dates, when is the best time to talk about sex? The first date? Only if the topic arises?
- What sexual limits should be placed on dates between unmarried individuals—what's acceptable? What's not?
- What's the role of a church's singles ministry? Is it to facilitate or arrange dates?
- Is dating your spouse once per month the right frequency?

Why Embrace Abstinence?

A former surgeon general of the United States made the following statement during a recent public gathering: "I really look at abstinence-only education as almost child abuse...they have all of these feelings and hormones raging, and we've not equipped them with the tools to make good decisions (Dr. Jocelyn Elders, State Journal Register, Springfield, IL, May 14, 2008)." The noted doctor added that she wants "abstinence until marriage, but we look at our society and we know that's not happening. Eighty to 90 percent of people have engaged in sex before marriage."

Many who heard her comments were turned off by the surrender mentality expressed, and especially the child-abuse comparison. Her statements imply that Christians, who teach abstinence before marriage, are somehow psychologically abusing their children and ill-equipping them for the society in which they live. On the contrary, Christians who teach abstinence before marriage are giving their children the benefit of

God's standard for their lives. God's standards do not ill-equip us, but if followed, they strengthen us to stand against whatever immoral, societal beliefs are the flavor of the day.

Society's sexual standards are forever changing. What was sexually taboo a few generations ago is now commonplace and readily accepted. But God's baseline principles of moral action and belief do not vacillate. He stated in one scripture, "I am the Lord, I change not" (Malachi 3:6), forthrightly declaring the constancy of his precepts. What the Bible taught about sexual behavior in ancient times is still relevant today.

Responsible church leaders, teachers, and parents should advocate teaching all Christians about contemporary sexual practices. Church leaders should do this while also teaching God's plan for our sexual lives. Christians are expected to operate in the world, though not "of the world" (John 17:14); so we must be aware of what is taking place around us in order to better teach what is appropriate and to warn against what is wrong. We should give our children and our parishioners an overview of how the world behaves and its sexual norms. It is not necessary for child or even adult Christians to know the intimate details of all the debauchery that occurs in our society.

Many Christians fall into the trap of immersing themselves in sex-laden literature, TV, and other media, under the guise of entertaining and educating themselves and wanting to be in the know. Such reading and viewing habits are a slippery slope to a lifestyle that is outside God's will. Once individuals become mesmerized by immoral sexual media, mimicking that media is not far behind. For this reason, an overview should be sufficient. The Bible admonishes us in Psalm chapter one to avoid the advice, instruction, and opinions of the world, because ultimately those ungodly ways are unstable and "shall perish" (verse six). Additionally, Titus 2:12 instructs us that "denying ungodliness and worldly lusts, we should live soberly, righteously, and godly in this present world."

Therefore, to be on solid, moral ground, Christians should teach abstinence, but should teach *abstinence preferentially.* The Christian stance should be a matter of personal inclination and God-inspired choice; it should not be a position of ignorance. Christians should seek full knowledge about matters of human sexuality, but simultaneously acquaint themselves with God's plan for managing that sexuality. God's plan is not inferior to the world's plan; it is just very different from the world's plan, calling us to a high and decent lifestyle. Preferential abstinence provides information, but then advocates a godly lifestyle over an immoral one.

Christians, however, must be careful about the timing of such teaching and the setting in which it takes place. There is no hard and fast rule about when a child should be taught about sexual abstinence and/or celibacy. Certainly if a child is being frequently exposed to sexual images and messages and is stimulated by, or has questions about these images, abstinence teaching should take place. Without question, if a child is showing interest in the opposite sex and is either courting or wanting to date, then abstinence education should take place. Each parent must be watchful and attuned to their child's sexual signals and behaviors. This sense of timing requires a healthy dose of godly wisdom.

The Bible is filled with scriptures calling Christians to abstinence before marriage, and describes fornication as one of the rampant sins of our society. Ephesians 5:3 is a classic example of God's wishes about this sin: "But fornication, and all uncleanness, or covetousness, let it not be once named among you, as becometh saints."

Fornication was defined and discussed earlier. Abstinence is the act or practice of refraining from indulging an appetite or desire, especially for sexual intercourse. One can be celibate, yet not want to be sexually abstinent—the celibacy being a matter of circumstance and not choice.

Abstinence is not a requirement for Christianity, at least not for those who are married. Maintaining celibate lives is something God expects of single Christians only. Many religious groups require abstinence of all its leading practitioners. Other faith traditions have made abstinence a *sine qua non* for members of clergy. This imposed celibacy is a pollution of Paul's written instruction to the Corinthians: "It is good for a man not to touch a woman" (1 Corinthians 7:1). Imposed celibacy is a difficult discipline to follow, and recent media disclosures of sexual misdeeds by unmarried clergy members should be proof enough for all.

Paul was speaking in 1 Corinthians 7:1 of individual preference or leaning. Paul's words in this passage meant that when a man or woman chooses to be abstinent as a sacrifice to God and as a way of devoting themselves full time to his service, without the necessity of maintaining a sexual relationship with a spouse, *it is good*! *It is good*, but it is not mandated. *It is good* because any concentrated, wholehearted commitment to God is praiseworthy. Those Christians who choose a celibate lifestyle will likely be more attentive to Christ and his teachings because they don't have to divide their attention between God and a sexual relationship with a spouse.

There are many single men and women in the church who are celibate, abstaining from sexual relations because of religious beliefs. Many of these individuals want to be in a dating relationship or to be married, but have not found the right partner. They abstain from sexual relations because they want to be true to God's directions that his followers should keep their bodies free from fornication. Such celibacy is to be praised because it comes from selflessness and sacrifice. These celibate Christians have given up much to maintain a close walk with the Lord, and they are deserving of our prayerful support.

Several men and women come to Christianity after having had active sex lives; many of these individuals bear the physical and mental scars of their sexual indiscretions. While vestiges of their former sex lives may be issues to be dealt with going forward, God's saving grace cleanses such individuals of all their past sin and spiritually makes them as clean and virginal as fresh-fallen snow. "Therefore, if any man [or woman] be in Christ, he is a new creature; old things are passed away; behold, all things are become new," (2 Corinthians 5:17).

Let's not be subtle about this matter. The world is literally carried away by attention to its carnal appetites. Sex and sexual images permeate all we see and do in this nation. The societal battle between sexual promiscuity and sexual propriety was lost by Christians ages ago. Satan rules this worldly roost, insofar as erotic expression is concerned and his influence is spread throughout the earth.

Christians are called upon to advocate for truth in this world by holding God's principles high. Just because the majority of those around us have given themselves over to sin, does not mean we also should acquiesce. We are God's *remnant*, or at least we should be striving to be. We should not wink at the world's depravity or fail to preach against its sins. God calls Christians to take a vocal position against sin in general and fornication in particular. The Psalmist asks, "Who shall rise up for me against the evildoers? Or who will stand up for me against the workers of iniquity?" (Psalm 94:16). Shout loudly, "I will stand, Lord; by your grace, I will stand!"

Summary Points:

- Abstinence is a God-ordained practice for single Christians; it is the way he wants us to live our lives prior to marriage.
- If in the past we sinned sexually, but now are saved, God gives us a new beginning, and we can embrace abstinence from the point of our salvation forward.
- The Christian who is abstinent should not be ashamed, but as appropriate, should testify of this sacrifice to God out of love for him and his ways.

Discussion Questions:

- Should abstinence education be accompanied by other forms of sex education? Explain your answer.
- What are the main elements of the *abstinence preferentially* plan?
- Do you think church pastors/leaders should be celibate? Explain your answer.
- Why is abstinence and a life free from fornication not regularly taught in today's churches?
- What is a *remnant*, and how does the word apply to those who would teach abstinence?
- If a Christian has already been sexually active, where would abstinence fit into their lives?
- Are there some sexual indiscretions that are just too awful to forgive?

Can We Show Our Nakedness?

The human body is a fascinating work of creation. Only an omnipotent, omniscient God could have fashioned our insides so skillfully and given us life. The skin he chose to cover and protect us is no less elaborative and evocative. God's love of beauty is nowhere more evident than in our outer appearances. Look at the faces and physiques of the people around you—their skin tones, the shape, and the placement of their appendages. What a marvelous love of beauty God must have and he routinely demonstrates it in the countenance and structure of individuals.

God's original plan for the happiness and sanctity of humanity was an excellent one and it is unfortunate we defied and usurped it almost from the very beginning, even in the realm of nudity. Bear in mind that in the beginning, nakedness was the order of the day. Scripture informs us: "And they were both naked, the man and his wife, and were not ashamed" (Genesis 2:25). The original world was a perfect place with ideal weather, work environment, and no wardrobe envy. It was only following the introduction of sin into that world that the unclothed body became an object of concern and embarrassment.

The first humans' apprehension about their bodies was not because nakedness is an inherently negative state, but because the first couple recognized they had gone against the will of God. The moment the natural "eyes of them both were opened" (Genesis 3:7), they simultaneously lost their spiritual covering and noticed their naked bodies. The first couple disobeyed God, overstepping the boundaries he had declared. The first thing they saw during this eye-opening experience was their nudity, and an immediate cover-up began. It is little wonder that ever since, some humans, psychologically, have had difficulty with the unclothed image.

The word *nakedness* is mentioned in the King James Version of the Bible fifty-seven times; *naked* is mentioned forty-seven times. The contextual use of these words can be very confusing to Christians, especially recognizing the shame experienced early on by Adam and Eve standing nude before their God, later coupled with the mortification of Shem and Japheth (Genesis chapter nine) when they discovered their father Noah uncovered. In most biblical instances, the word *naked* is used in a disapproving way. In Leviticus chapter eighteen, there are a litany of pronouncements reminding you to not *uncover the nakedness* of this or that person—*thy father… thy mother… thy father's wife … thy sister,* etc. Nakedness is definitely portrayed as a private matter.

In the Bible, to be naked is to be uncovered—naturally and spiritually, and to be uncovered is an undesirable state. God is meant to be our spiritual covering, and we must recognize and seek a relationship with him where he is sovereign and the over-arching force in our lives. Christians must keep in mind the circumstances under which the term *nakedness* is used in the Bible and consider all scriptural guidance before coming to a negative conclusion about this subject.

When you add the biblical warnings about nakedness to the conservative, societal teaching over the ages and our media-twisted body self-images, it is a wonder we Christians ever take our clothes off in front of one another. In Eden, we forfeited our innocent, blissful existence and for a time were literally and figuratively exposed. Since that time, God has expected that we will keep our natural *nakedness* (genitalia and other privy parts) covered in almost all circumstances. Exodus 20:26 is but one of many verses that speaks to this edict—"Neither shalt thou go up by steps into mine altar, that thy nakedness be not discovered thereon," which is to say, don't put yourself in a position where someone of the general public can see your privy parts, while at the altar or anywhere else.

In church gatherings, it is important that men and women not dress in a manner that is too revealing and therefore distracting. At such meetings, the attention should be on the gathering and its purpose, not on an individual's outfit. Sometimes churchgoers wear clothing that is too tight, too skimpy, and shows too much skin. While doing such is not true nakedness, the effect can still be titillating and divert attention from the sacred to the sexual. Beyond the privy parts, societal norms tend to dictate what other bodily areas should be covered and when. Culture, climate, and personal preference heavily impact how we dress ourselves. Consequently, there is wide variance in our apparel.

It is interesting that non-Christian society has very few hang-ups about showing their bodies in public. With each passing year that secular group moves societal norms toward less clothing in public and readily shows more flesh to the masses. This worldly group could care less about having their bodies exposed. Even so, Christ-followers must not be like the world in this matter. Christians should not revel in ostentatious, public displays of their bodies. The Bible teaches that discretion is a desirable character trait (see Titus 2:5: "Be discreet … that the Word of God be not blasphemed" and Genesis 41:33: "Look out a man discreet and wise, and set him over the land"). This having been said, Christians should not be ashamed of their bodies either, and should be willing to expose those bodies under the right circumstances, to the right person. The right person is your spouse; the right circumstances are moments of privacy between the two of you. Remember, Scripture declares that you are "wonderfully made" (Psalm 139:14), and you should be glad about it and unashamed.

Are you old enough to recall the days when women and men of the church intentionally dressed discreetly and simply? They were proud of their toned-down attire and saw it as a reflection of their desire to be holy and set apart from the world. Nowadays it is very difficult to distinguish a Christian from a non-Christian on the basis of attire. Again, Titus 2:5 encourages women especially to be *discreet, chaste*. For many women and men, there is nothing as sexy as a member of the opposite sex who covers hers or his body, fashionably and tastefully, still leaving a good bit to the imagination.

Now for a direct answer to the question: Can we show our nakedness? The answer is "Yes!" Yes, please show your nakedness to your spouse. Uncover yourself fully and experience increased intimacy for having done so. Nakedness is only un-Christian when done in public, before eyes that should not see and have no right to see. Showing this special view of your body, with all the emotional exposure that accompanies doing so, is something reserved for your spouse and for none other. Now, if your spouse doesn't want to see your naked body, the two of you may want to discuss that matter further. Short of the rare circumstance where one or both of you do not want to see the other's exposed flesh, bare your body and your sexual spirit before your spouse, who is your lover—all to the glory of God.

Summary Points:

- The naked body is a beautiful creation *wonderfully made* by God.
- Christians should not display their nakedness in public and should be discreet in their attire.
- It is acceptable and often pleasing to show your nakedness to your spouse, but it is not mandatory.

Discussion Questions:

- If nakedness is such a good thing, why does the Bible speak of it in negative ways, so often?
- Shouldn't you be able to see your spouse naked whenever you please?
- How should church congregations handle the situation where someone attends a meeting with too much flesh exposed?
- What is the main reason people do not want to show their nakedness?
- Does discretion have a certain look, or is it a state of the mind and heart?
- What about a nudist beach, camp, or colony; is this an acceptable place for a Christian to visit?

Does It Matter If I Masturbate?

Men and women have been touching and stimulating themselves sexually since first discovering their genitalia. This kind of sex activity is a natural part of childhood exploration, adolescent excitation, and is often carried into adulthood with little diminished frequency. Masturbation is the stimulation or manipulation of one's own or another's genitals, usually to orgasm. This practice is not to be confused with *nocturnal emissions*, or *wet dreams*—ejaculations that occur spontaneously while one is asleep. In the not too distant past, Christians were condemned for such night-time discharges and expected to repent of this *sin*. But in truth, most members of the human race are unable to control dreams, or the physical emissions and expulsions that happen while sleeping, so these happenings could hardly be sinful.

Masturbation, on the other hand, is intentional. Research has shown that during adolescence many more males than females masturbate. As a result of these repeated manipulations, it is thought that males become more genital-oriented in their sexual practices, whereas females can achieve satisfaction from a broader array of stimuli.

Masturbation is a controversial topic, and the performance of it has gotten a decidedly negative rap over the years. Many disapproving myths have built up around the practice, and at different points in our history, naysayers have tried to eliminate or treat the so called *sin* of masturbation with electro-shock therapy, castration, cauterization, and a varied array of restraining devices. Even in the face of such past ignorance and cruelty, masturbation is likely as prolific today as at any time in history. The practice of masturbation is better understood by contemporary society (although unevenly discussed in open conversation) and has been touted to have some physically beneficial effects.

Although claims are still disputed, articles in the *Journal of the American Medical Association* and *Sexual-Reproductive* (both in April 2004), and the *New Scientist* (July 2003), suggest that frequent ejaculation has a protective effect against prostate disease. Frequent ejaculators also experience lowered blood pressure (at least transiently). Blood pressure is known to rise during the plateau phase of the human sexual response cycle (see the book *Human Sexual Response*) and peak during orgasm and ejaculation. The phenomenon of post-ejaculatory, lowered blood pressure is evident during the physiologic refractory period. When humans are sexually refractory immediately following orgasm, their blood pressures go from the elevated state of sexual arousal, to normal or low levels.

W.G. Robinson-McNeese, M.D.

Women and men masturbate for various reasons; some common reasons are because they have no sex partner, or they have not been fully satisfied during sexual intercourse and want more. Some people masturbate in preparation for sexual intercourse to decrease anxiety and increase performance (masturbation causes the penis to be less sensitive and therefore less prone to premature ejaculations). It is thought that the second and subsequent male ejaculations, over a relatively brief period, take longer to occur, so men believe masturbating before coitus will increase their staying power. Others masturbate themselves or their partner during sexual intercourse as a way of increasing pleasure.

What the Bible purportedly mentions about the subject of masturbation is often misinterpreted, especially the story in Genesis 38 regarding Judah's instructions to his son Onan. In this story, Onan is directed to impregnate his older brother's wife Tamar. Judah's directions to Onan were in keeping with the law of the time that was meant to assure the family lineage of an older brother who died leaving behind male siblings. Onan's older brother Er, due to acts of wickedness, had been slain by God.

"Raise up seed to thy brother" (verse eight), Onan was told by Judah. Onan, however, knowing that any child born of his union with his brother's widow would legally be a credit to his brother and not to himself, decided to foil the plan. Scripture tells, "When he went in unto his brother's wife, that he spilled it [the seed] on the ground . . . and the thing which he did displeased the Lord: wherefore he slew him also" (verses nine and ten).

Some theologians have mislabeled Onan's spilling of his seed as masturbation, suggesting that Onan went in to his brother's wife and in defiance of his father's directions masturbated rather than copulated. There is nothing in these scriptures to suggest that Onan was involved in anything other than copulation. If Onan was just going to [masturbate] *spill his seed* inside the tent (ostensibly until there was no more ejaculate to impregnate Tamar), there was no reason for Onan to go in to be with his brother's wife; he could have just found a quiet place elsewhere and masturbated until there was no more ejaculate. Plus, if Onan went into the tent solely to masturbate, Tamar would have witnessed this act and would have had to be part of a conspiracy to trick Judah. Those who misconstrue these passages go on to deduce that since God slew Onan, he did so because of Onan's masturbatory sin.

A more accurate interpretation of the story is that Onan practiced *coitus interruptus* and stopped what he was doing—copulating, secretly and in time enough for ejaculation to occur outside the vagina (the spilling of the seed). What angered God is that Onan did not obey his father Judah's directions, nor did he obey the established law of the time. *Onanism*, therefore, has incorrectly been labeled masturbation and a sin because of a misinterpretation of this Bible story. Onanism could more accurately be described as the sin of disregard for the rules of your heavenly Father, your earthly father, and the laws of man.

Other scriptures that erroneously have been thought to speak against masturbation are 1 Corinthians 6:9–10. In these scriptures Paul points out that the "unrighteous shall not inherit the kingdom of God." Paul goes on to be more specific and gives a list of ten life circumstances that are unacceptable to the Master: "Neither fornicators, nor idolaters, nor adulterers, nor effeminate, nor abusers of themselves with mankind [not the complete list]." Paul explains that none of the aforementioned "shall inherit the kingdom of God."

Again, some theologians have sighted in on the phrase *abusers of themselves* as describing those who masturbate, since masturbation is often expressed as self-abuse of the genitals. The often-vigorous manipulation of, tugging on and stroking of the penis that occurs during masturbation was thought to be an abuse of that body part.

A more broadly accepted interpretation of the First Corinthians scriptures under discussion, has *abusers of themselves* meaning the sins of sodomy between two males and/or sodomy performed on a boy (more than one well-recognized Bible commentator—the IVP Background Commentary interprets the phrase to mean *homosexuals* and Matthew Henry interprets the phrase as *Sodomites*—agrees with this interpretation). Paul rightly speaks against sodomitic sins in these passages, not against masturbation. Indeed, the Bible offers no direction on the practice of self-stimulation. Nonetheless, Christians by and large are ashamed when they masturbate, or they masturbate not at all.

Since the Bible does not specifically offer guidance about this practice, this book offers that masturbation is not a sin and can be carried out with only a few caveats: (1) Mutual masturbation is not acceptable outside of marriage; (2) No married person should be driven to masturbate because their spouse is unwilling to participate in sexual intercourse; and (3) Masturbation should not be tied to the viewing of pornographic materials.

Mutual masturbation occurs when two individuals in concert use their hands, other body parts, and/or devices to stimulate themselves and/or their partner; this type shared masturbation is for married couples.

Many unmarried Christian couples have turned to mutual masturbation as a way to satisfy their sexual urgings, but still avoid copulation. Such couples deceive themselves, reasoning that because no copulation has taken place, they have not broken God's laws. When unmarried Christians participate in mutual masturbation, they are adhering to the letter of the law by not copulating, but totally ignoring its spirit. The Bible's stance against copulation is not just against a penis being inserted into a vagina, but also against the kind of premature physical and emotional intimacy that accompanies such sexual practices. God wants couples to reserve the intimacy of copulation and masturbation for the marriage bed. There is no way two people can participate in mutual masturbation without crossing over into a type of intimacy that is reserved for matrimony. It is highly unlikely that a couple participating in mutual masturbation won't over time progress to other forms of sexual intercourse outside the bounds of appropriate Christian dating, especially coitus—once again, that slippery slope.

The second point mentioned above is a reiteration of the principle of *due benevolence* (talked about in an earlier chapter). No spouse should be compelled to masturbate because their sex partner is unwilling to participate in coitus, or some other acceptable, sexual substitute, except *with consent for a time*. It is okay if spouses want to masturbate in concert or in solitude, but neither of those masturbatory episodes should take place because one of the partners refuses copulation or other sexual intercourse.

Stipulation number three accentuates the point that masturbation should be a private matter for an individual alone, or an individual and spouse. The practice should be a way of achieving solitary, sexual release, or heightening a spouse's pleasure, and should not involve the viewing of obscene material either before, during, or after. Pornography should not be within the purview of Christians.

Finally, while the hands are the usual tools used to masturbate, there is no reason other objects and devices cannot be used, but be as careful as you are creative in these exceptionally sensitive erogenous zones. The goal of masturbation is erotic release and enjoyment, not injury. And while masturbation will not cause hair to grow on the palms of your hands, or your hands to fall off, or your eyes to cross, Christians should not spend such inordinate amounts of time in this practice that it becomes a fixation. If you simply must fixate on something, let it not be on sexual things, or the things of this world, but on Jesus, who is the Christ.

Summary Points:

- Masturbation is an acceptable form of sexual release, but should not become a mainstay of the Christian lifestyle.
- Masturbation should be practiced alone, or with your spouse, and not urged on by the viewing of pornographic materials.
- No spouse should be compelled to masturbate because their partner will not provide other sexual intercourse.

Discussion Questions:

- While it is true masturbation will not cause your hand to fall off, can it be practiced to excess? Please explain.
- Reportedly there are some physical benefits from masturbation; what physical harm can come from the practice?
- What is *Onanism*? What was the sin of Onan?
- If sexual manipulation doesn't end in orgasm, has masturbation actually occurred?
- Do you agree that men are more genital-oriented than women, or is that statement just a myth?
- What is the meaning of the phrase, *erogenous zone*? Where are such zones located?

Sexual
Acts

What Is Sexual Intercourse?

One could easily fill a page with common-use terms for sexual intercourse. Every sexually aware teen and adult owns a few—some fit for public consumption and others best left for private use. Christians are not exempt from this conversational behavior. We discuss the topic so often that we've developed pet terms, phrases, passwords, gestures, and signals to make certain others know what we're talking about. Therefore, it is interesting that this often bandied about phrase—sexual intercourse—must be defined; delineated here because men and women have begun splitting hairs about what qualifies as sexual intercourse and what does not.

The public dances around the phrase and manipulates its meaning to justify questionable sexual practices. Christian couples excuse themselves by thinking, "Yes, we did this or that, but we didn't have sexual intercourse, so we're all right in God's sight. After all, we didn't break the rules; we didn't have sex." Such thinking is nonsense!

To have *intercourse* with another means to have dealings with them—an exchange of some sort usually involving communication. To have sexual intercourse with another, therefore, means to have sexual dealings and exchange—a form of sexual communication. Sexual intercourse is not confined to penile penetration of the vagina. Even Webster's dictionary describes sexual intercourse as *any human genital contact*. The dictionary then goes on to add: *especially contact that involves insertion of the penis into the vagina followed by orgasm; coitus, copulation; a joining together*.

Sexual intercourse is not confined to *human genital contact*, and it comes in many forms—not just vaginal penetration. Oral sex, hand sex, phone sex, rubbing sex, hugging sex, grinding sex, kissing sex—all these and more are forms of sexual intercourse. Give it whatever pet name you like, if you engage in an act of sexual stimulation with another, then you are engaging in a form of sexual intercourse (communication) and have placed yourself somewhere on the sexual intercourse continuum.

Scripture unquestionably speaks against one form of sexual intercourse—fornication! Fornication is most specifically *copulation between two persons not married to one another*, but includes any form of deeply intimate sexual interplay with someone who is not your spouse. The word fornication has Latin derivation—*fornicationem*—and means arch or vaulted chamber. One can fairly easily make the connection between a vaulted chamber and the shape of the female vagina. Plus, it is also thought that ancient Romans would meet prostitutes in the underground vaulted chambers of cities, so the activities that took place there came to be known as fornication.

The Bible teaches: "Now the body is not for fornication, but for the Lord, and the Lord for the body" (1 Corinthians 6:13). "Flee fornication" (verse eighteen). "For this is the will of God, even your sanctification, that ye should abstain from fornication" (1 Thessalonians 4:3).

While Scripture is unequivocal in condemning fornication, many Christians are just the opposite, and waffle on this most important topic. Large numbers of religious converts have fallen prey to this enticement. They dabble in fornication, but still direct activities of a congregation and by doing so flaunt this sexual act before God and company. They are shacking up while still serving in church auxiliaries, and unfortunately many church leaders turn a blind eye to this behavior. Fornication diminishes the testimony and warps the witness of Christians. Because our society is so obviously sexual, hordes of pastors have given up preaching and teaching against fornication, permitting its unchecked spread. Apparently, such pastors are afraid of losing members if they speak against fornication, so they do not. God is not pleased! Fornication is not acceptable!

Outside of marriage, all forms of sexual intercourse are problematic, and most of them transparently wrong and sinful. Think of it as a sexual spectrum with handholding on one end of the spectrum and a *hand-job* on the other. Not too many reasonable Christian leaders would speak against handholding, but most would agree that giving and/or receiving a *hand-job* should be confined to marriage. Where we struggle is on the sexual practices that lie somewhere between these two; or in other words, "Can we do this and that?"

Sexual intercourse in its myriad forms, is figuratively and literally a slippery slope. Christians may start with a gentle caress and kiss on the cheek, but in the presence of surging hormones and growing passion, these practices can easily progress to heavy petting, pseudo-sex (any form of sexual intercourse that helps you achieve sexual satisfaction or orgasmic relief, short of copulation) and coitus. Acceptable, Christian sexual interplay outside of marriage should be kept at the most benign, minimally stimulating level, as we seek to preserve our sanctity and morality. Instead we seem to aim for sexual interplay that causes arousal. We want to be turned on!

Sexual arousal in healthy men usually results in penile erection and increased blood flow and tumescence of the male genitalia. Aroused women also experience increased genital blood flow, erection of nipples, and increased lubrication of the vagina (there are many other signs of arousal). Men and women know when they have become sexually aroused, and while there are many physiological responses that happen to all humans at these times, we also display individualistic and idiosyncratic behaviors when we are sexually turned on.

Unmarried Christians should avoid situations where they are sexually aroused, because these situations can easily lead to pseudo-sex and/or copulation. When Christians are engaging in sexual routines that get them all hot and bothered, they have entered a danger zone and should think about backing away from the relationship altogether, backing away at least long enough to cool off, or consummating it legally in the sight of God—marriage.

Sexual intercourse, therefore, is any form of sexual interplay between a man and woman—boy or girl; it comes in many flavors, pops up all the time in relationships, and needs to be controlled if we are to be pleasing in God's sight. Since the human body is designed by God to be sexually desirable and responsive, we cannot spin this siren instrument but then expect no seductive music to come forth. Therefore, Christians who want to remain chaste must carefully avoid situations where sexual arousal is the planned result. And Christians must be prepared to walk away, nay, run away from the situations if the need arises.

God's directive is this: "Every one of you should know how to possess his vessel in sanctification and in honour" (1 Thessalonians 4:4). The *vessel* being described here is your body and its sexual nature. This discipline of our sexual nature is an expression of how much we love God; how much we are willing to sacrifice for him; how spiritually mature we are.

A scripture that gets right to the crux of this matter encourages: "Present your bodies, a living sacrifice, holy, acceptable unto God;" this scripture points out that abstaining from sexual intercourse is the deliberate subjugation of natural sexual desires and longings to faithfully follow the teachings of Christ. Such sacrifice is the "reasonable service" expected of us by God (Romans 12:1). Through our continual attitude of sacrifice and (most importantly) with God's help, we are able to preserve our chastity.

Summary Points:

- Sexual intercourse is any form of sexual interplay between males and females and involves a wide spectrum of practices.

- Fornication is not an acceptable part of the Christian life; there is no excuse or justification for sexual immorality.
- Pseudo-sex is an attempt to skirt the biblical command against fornication—especially copulation, by engaging in other forms of orgasmic release (with a partner); it is just as unacceptable.

Discussion Questions:

- How can unmarried individuals tell when they have crossed the line into sexual immorality—fornication?
- Does sexual arousal during dating occur less slowly in a devout Christian than in a non-Christian?
- How can unmarried Christians change the dating model from working to be sexually turned on, to working to get to know one another better on a social level?
- Copulation is certainly *sexual intercourse*; what are some other sexual practices that fit into that *intercourse* category?
- How did *shacking up* come to be such a prominent, well-tolerated practice in the contemporary church? What can be done about it?
- Is coitus acceptable between an unmarried couple if marriage plans are imminent?

W.G. Robinson-McNeese, M.D.

Is the Missionary Position Mandatory?

There are several scriptures in the Bible that speak of men copulating with women. Many of these scriptures use the phrase *lay with* to describe the sexual act. Following are three examples:

"Now Eli was very old, and heard all that his sons did unto all Israel; and how they lay with the women that assembled at the door of the tabernacle of the congregation" (1 Samuel 2:22). In this instance, Eli's sons, Hophni and Phinehas, by copulating with the women who came to the tabernacle, were operating outside the bounds of decency and the law of God. As a direct result of their copulatory sin, the sons' deaths were foretold, and the two were later slain during a Hebrew battle with the Philistines.

A second scripture deals with the conception and subsequent birth of Solomon (the story of David and Bathsheba is dealt with in greater detail later in this book): "And David comforted Bathsheba his wife, and went in unto her, and lay with her: and she bare a son, and he called his name Solomon: and the Lord loved him" (2 Samuel 12:24).

The final example, also from the Old Testament, outlines part of the penalty against a man who has sexual intercourse with a virgin: "Then the man that lay with her shall give unto the damsel's father fifty shekels of silver, and she shall be his wife; because he hath humbled her, he may not put her away all his days" (Deuteronomy 22:29).

Because of these scriptures and many others like them, some have taken this phrase, "lay with," to be a description of and command about how coitus is to be performed in a Christian relationship. These literalists assert that copulation should be carried out only when two people are lying down, otherwise the act is unseemly. Such a narrow interpretation of the phrase is usually accompanied by instruction that the missionary position is the only appropriate and acceptable position for sexual intercourse when two lovers are lying down.

Such assertions are wrong. The phrase *lay with* is merely a euphemism of the time used to describe a sex act, and not a pronouncement about how that sex act should be carried out. The Bible does not sanction a particular sexual position for copulation, and neither does this book. You are left to your own imaginations to come up with positions for sexual intercourse.

It should come as no surprise to you to learn that the missionary position of sexual intercourse has been practiced, recorded, and described for as long as humans have been copulating. By the same reasoning, it is logical that other copulatory positions have been utilized just as often. It is the nature of humans to experiment and create in sexual situations, and there are probably more sexual positions attempted than any of us would care to conceptualize. The Bible gives no direction on these myriad positions, but there are a plethora of books to be had if you really want to explore the subject.

This chapter highlights the missionary position only because through myth that sexual position is tied to Christianity, with many believing that early Christians were admonished to adhere to this posture and only this posture during times of love-making. The position was labeled *missionary*, because early Christian missionaries who carried the gospel message to foreign cultures often encountered sex practices that were blatantly raw and thought to be unseemly. The more civilized missionaries reportedly instructed native converts to adhere to the missionary position only, and to abandon rear-entry, woman-on-top, and other copulation poses that were more earthy, and therefore unacceptable.

The following description of the missionary position is lifted verbatim from *Wikipedia*, and is mentioned here only to further explain the pose, and to dismiss the idea that Christians must have sex one way and one way only.

> The missionary position is a male-superior (man on top) coitus position in which the woman lies on her back and the partners face each other. Variations of the position allow different degrees of vaginal tightness, clitoral stimulation, depth of penetration, participation on the part of the woman, and likelihood and speed of orgasm. These variations may involve the woman resting her feet on the bed,

lifting them up high into the air, or wrapping them around her partner; or placing one or more pillows under the woman's hips. The missionary position is the most commonly-used position in the United States...The missionary position is often preferred by couples who enjoy its romantic qualities afforded by copious skin-to-skin contact and opportunities to look into each other's eyes and kiss and caress each other. The position is also believed to be a good position for procreation.

http://en.wikipedia.org/wiki/Missionary_sex_position

Wikipedia

As mentioned in the introduction to this book, this writing is not meant to be a sex-manual, and will not describe other sexual positions in the same detail as above. You are encouraged, however, to position yourselves for pleasure. Remember the underlying premise of this book, that the marriage bed, floor, table, etc. is *undefiled* and the only forbidden practice is sodomy, extramarital, and group sex. So, purchase a copy of a sex manual if you wish, and use whatever position gives you pleasure and fits your physical abilities. Don't hurt one another, and don't tear up the place too much, but otherwise go for it! You must use common sense and good judgment as you decide how to arrange your bodies for sexual interplay.

Don't forget, though, variety often is the spice of life where sexual matters are concerned. After listening to many married couples discuss sexual variety, or the lack thereof, this conclusion follows: Sexually, we like what we're doing, the way we're doing it, until we try it a different way, then we often become more receptive to the change. Sexual gymnastics and contortions are not the playground for all, but many couples are very comfortable in this arena. Enjoy this corporal creativity while you can. And with your God-given spouse, turn your sexual imaginations loose!

Summary Points:

- When the Bible mentions the phrase *lay with*, it is not dictating a specific copulation position.
- The missionary position of sexual intercourse is not mandated by the Bible.
- Christians are free to practice whatever sexual positions they might imagine as long as they are not engaging in extramarital sex, group sex, or sodomy.

Discussion Questions:

- Why is the missionary position thought to be good for procreation? Aren't other positions just as good for getting pregnant?
- Any additional thoughts about what was distasteful to missionaries about rear-entry, woman-on-top, and other sexual positions beyond the *missionary* one?
- How should you bring up the subject with your spouse if you want to try a different position for love-making? What's the best spousal response to such a request?

- What should be the limiting factor(s) for sexual intercourse positions for you and your spouse?
- Are any and all sex manuals acceptable for Christian instruction? Explain.

What
About
Cunnilingus?

Cunnilingus is oral stimulation of the vulva or clitoris using the lips, mouth, and/or tongue. The word has a Latin derivation, with *cunnus* meaning *vulva* and *lingus* meaning *to lick*. As with most sexual practices, variations on the cunnilingus theme have developed over the years, and its practitioners use an assortment of positions and aids when engaged in this exceptionally intimate form of sexual intercourse. Cunnilingus has been around for ages and is another sexual custom likely as old as sexual interplay itself.

This type oral sex is thought to be most prevalent in arenas of higher, more complex civilization. While sexual intercourse will always be pleasurable, simpler cultures tend to see copulation as a way to sustain the species and extend the cultural norms. On the other hand, advanced civilizations move away from sexual practices aimed primarily at procreation to those aimed more at pleasure. While cunnilingus may certainly be a prelude to procreation, usually reproduction is not the primary objective of cunnilingus.

Some modern day sexologists teach that no human copulation should ever occur without oral-genital fore-play having taken place. One could argue whether this current age represents a period of higher civilization, but most people in the secular world believe it does, and cunnilingus is very prevalent in the secular world.

This form of vaginal stimulation is a mainstay practice in some eastern religions where it is believed that female vaginal fluids are the essence of life. Cunnilingus permits the male practitioner to deliberately take these fluids into his body, rather than have them lost to the surroundings. Admittedly, this is an interesting eastern religious belief, but whether in the north, south, east, or west, and religious leaning notwithstanding, cunnilingus is a widespread sexual practice.

In the Christian world, there still lingers the belief that the genitalia are for procreation, and maybe for pleasure, but certainly not for pleasure derived from mouth to genital contact. Consequently, cunnilingus, if practiced at all, is almost never talked about among Christians.

Please remember the underlying principle of this book: *the marriage bed is undefiled!* To wit, if your husband gains pleasure from orally stimulating you in this manner, and you also are receptive to his advances, then you should practice this form of sexual intercourse without guilt or shame. The Bible does not explicitly speak about cunnilingus; actually, Scripture is thought to be silent on the matter (though some say not).

Some theologians, when discussing this oral sex topic, will cite a passage from the "Letter of Barnabas" that commands Christians to *not commit iniquity with the mouth*. The "Letter of Barnabas" is a manuscript from an early Christian literature collection, ascribed to the apostolic fathers, but thought by most Bible scholars to be the product of an anonymous author. Two things about this passage: First, it is not a passage from the Bible—our authority for these writings. Secondly, *iniquity with the mouth* speaks to those who participate in oral sex outside of marriage and not to those who practice it within the sacred confines of that union. The "Letter of Barnabas" (even if you choose to use it as an authority) is being misinterpreted in this instance and should not stand as an edict against cunnilingus, but rather an edict against illegitimate sexual sin of the oral type.

There is an often debated scripture in Song of Solomon 7:1–2 that reads as follows:

> How beautiful are thy feet with shoes, O prince's daughter! The joints of thy thighs are like jewels, the work of the hands of a cunning workman. Thy navel is like a round goblet which wanteth not liquor: thy belly is like a heap of wheat set about with lilies.

This verse is controversial only because Bible scholars disagree about the word *navel*, some arguing that the appropriate translation should have been vulva rather than *navel*. Following are a sampling of theories about verse two and its *navel* reference from some rather well-known commentators:

Barnes explains that the word *navel* refers to a woman's lap that is described as "a moon-shaped bowl where mixed wine faileth not." In the scripture, the bowl is filled to the brim with *liquor* signifying the heady, aromatic nature that can be characteristic of this part of the female anatomy. Recall how even the great Samson lost his strength and eventually his sight after Delilah lured him to the intoxicating experience of sleeping "upon her knees" (Judges 16:19). Here Barnes takes the biblical meaning away from the lone umbilicus to include all of a woman's pelvic region. [Barnes' Notes on the Old Testament, Quick Verse 2008, Version 12.0.2 (Dec 27, 2007 19:33:43)]

Keil and Delitzsch explain that the word in Hebrew means *pudenda*, the base word for pudendum. The pudendum is the human external genitalia, especially of the female. Surely the goblet spoken of in this example is a woman's vagina. [Keil and Delitzsch Commentary on the Old Testament, Quick Verse 2008, Version 12.0.2 (Dec 27, 2007 19:33:43)]

The New Commentary on the Whole Bible explains that the "bride's dance reveals her navel, which is decorated by rubies." This commentary goes on to explain how *Pope and Dillow* understand the word as a description of the vulva, "which is exposed in her naked dance before her husband." [The New Commentary on the Whole Bible: Old Testament Volume, Quick Verse 2008, Version 12.0.2 (Dec 27, 2007 19:33:43)]

The *Expositions of Holy Scripture* choose not to deal with this specific matter or the Song of Solomon at all, and *Matthew Henry* sees the writing as totally allegorical.

Those arguing in favor of the translation meaning vulva, go on to say that it makes no anatomical or amorous sense for the husband portrayed in this scripture, in the throes of passion, to progress upwards from a woman's feet to her thighs, then skip over her vagina, moving next to her navel, followed by her belly (especially since he goes to such great lengths to describe the joints of her thighs). These scholars question why this biblical husband, who seems to be erotically astute in all other areas, would not linger at, or at least speak about the woman's vagina, arguably a woman's most inviting part.

These theologians believe the scripture, properly translated, should read: *thy vulva is like a round goblet which wanteth not liquor.* They put forward that in this song the husband has described his wife as something good to eat and/or drink and his plan is to indulge heartily, orally stimulating every part of her body during the lovemaking ritual. But arguments over the translation notwithstanding, whichever word you pick—navel or vulva, *the marriage bed is undefiled.* And, if cunnilingus is for the two of you, then so be it.

Also, remember that cunnilingus carried out on a partner who has vaginal disease or poor hygiene can lead to a very distasteful experience, transmission of sexual diseases, and throat cancer. Spouses should be especially considerate of one another if they are going to practice this form of sexual intercourse, with the lion's share of the responsibility falling on the wife; and if all things are not physically in order and clean, couples should hold on this form of oral sex. Cunnilingus is one of the best reasons to practice the cleanliness habits talked about later in this book.

Do be aware that many of your Christian sisters and brothers would be appalled and repulsed by your participation in cunnilingus. The sexual routines found appealing by you and your spouse may be totally repugnant to another couple. One of the main objectives of the sexual encounter, however, is to please you and your spouse and—not others. So, what you do in your bedroom is no one else's business. Just stay within the boundaries of what is biblically permitted, if you want to "keep his commandments, and do those things that are pleasing in his sight" (1 John 3:20).

Summary Points:

- Cunnilingus, if practiced, is for married couples only, and close attention should be given to matters of timing and hygiene.
- Cunnilingus is one of the most intimate forms of sexual intercourse.

Discussion Questions:

- The Bible does not speak against cunnilingus; does the Bible speak for the practice?
- Some believe the Bible does describe and/or allude to an act of cunnilingus in Songs of Solomon chapter seven. What do you think?
- What is the "Letter of Barnabas;" are there other letters in this collection? What is its relevance to Christians concerning the oral sex issue?

- What is it about cunnilingus that makes it attractive to some? What makes it unattractive to others?
- What type sexually transmitted infections are spread through oral sex?
- How did the practice of cunnilingus get started?

Is
Fellatio
Okay?

If you've read this book to this point, the answer to the above question should be fairly obvious. Nonetheless, clarity on this topic is important. Fellatio is an acceptable practice for Christian, married couples!

Fellatio is oral stimulation performed on the male penis usually with the goal of inducing orgasm and/or semen ejaculation. The ejaculate is often swallowed during these episodes, though not necessarily. Male to male fellatio is not a Christian practice.

Fellatio is a derivative of the Latin word *fellare*, which means *to suck*. It is similar to cunnilingus, but with the husband's and wife's roles reversed. Also, it has a similar societal history. Because oral stimulation of the penis is correspondent to cunnilingus, it is acceptable for many of the same reasons already mentioned. There is no documented statement or inference about fellatio in the Bible.

Fellatio reportedly was prevalent in the court and kingdom of Ahab, the practice having been brought there by his wife Jezebel. Ahab married Jezebel:

> And it came to pass, as if it had been a light thing for him to walk in the sins of Jeroboam the son of Nebat, that he took to wife Jezebel, the daughter of Ethbaal, King of the Zidonians, and went and served Baal and worshipped him.
>
> (1 Kings 16:31)

After the marriage, he indulged his wife and began to permit many of the idolatrous ways of her homeland: "Thou sufferest that woman Jezebel, which calleth herself a prophetess, to teach and to seduce my servants to commit fornication, and to eat things sacrificed unto idols" (Revelation 2:20).

Reportedly, prostitutes of that day would paint their lips to resemble the colors of the inner folds of the vulva. Interested men were able to identify these fellatrices by the colorful lip display making their search for receptive women partners much easier. This painting of the lips is part of the origins of lipstick-wearing. Many modern day women do not know the origins of their lip rituals and make the application of lipstick a near daily routine. And just as modern day society has embraced the use of lipstick, it also has embraced the custom of fellatio. Fellatio, likely, has received its bad name because of its tie to prostitution and other forms of fornication. When the practice is carried out between husband and wife, there is no reason for guilt, shame, or disdain.

This book is written at a time when oral sex is being widely practiced in our society, especially by teenagers. Many teenagers and adults use oral sex as an alternative to copulation because of the sexual turn-on achieved, but also because there is no risk of pregnancy. Present day research suggests that half of U.S. teenagers have engaged in some form of oral sex by the time they complete high school.

Some Christian adults and teenagers have convinced themselves that cunnilingus and/or fellatio are not forms of sexual intercourse at all, and therefore are acceptable for Christian singles. These members of the secular and Christian community think oral sex is safer, and that it effectively keeps its practitioners from moral and medical contamination. Nothing could be further from the truth! Oral sex is a form of sexual intercourse that should be confined to the marital relationship. There is no sexual practice other than coitus that is as intimate. Sexual intercourse is not only defined by coitus. Sexual intercourse is any romantic physical interplay that occurs between couples. It is more a spectrum of events than a specific act.

It is self-deceptive and hypocritical to think we can put our mouths on one another's genitalia, rub our bodies against one another's in sweaty passion, probe privy areas with our fingers and other devices, bring one another to orgasm, but think we're somehow free from sexual intercourse and sin because no penis entered a vagina. Again, such thinking is nonsense! Sexual interplay beyond the superficial should be reserved for marriage. The type of intimacy that attends fellatio is for married couples, and not for just any individual who is able to produce a sexual response. Like it or not, that's the moral truth of it.

On the medical end of this subject, please know that most all sexually transmitted infections, including HIV/AIDS, can be transmitted through oral sex. Our society has recently developed an oral condom—a flexible barrier to prevent the transmission of some bodily fluids. Keep this in mind. If in your marital, oral sex-play you are at all concerned about the transmission of disease, you might want to use this devise, or forego fellatio altogether.

That being said, Christian female spouses may practice fellatio if it suits the wishes of the couple; the details and nuances of the ritual are appropriately left to the two of you.

Summary Points:

- Fellatio is an acceptable practice for Christian couples.
- Fellatio is not for teens or anyone else who is not married.
- At all times, strict attention to hygiene and the absence of disease should precede this practice.

Discussion Questions:

- Is fellatio a form of foreplay or an act unto itself?
- When oral sex is not part of a couple's sexual repertoire, how should the subject be brought up by one or the other partner?
- How are STIs transmitted during oral sex; doesn't the saliva kill the offending organisms?
- You have learned what signals lip-painting sent in ancient times; what is the message being sent today?
- Should Christians abstain from wearing lipstick because of the history mentioned above?

Is It Okay to Enjoy Orgasms?

Orgasms are special, and most people enjoy them! An orgasm is an often explosive emotional and physical release that is accompanied by a feeling of euphoria and/or ecstasy. An orgasm tends to occur at a climax point in sexual intercourse, often copulation, though it could happen with masturbation, oral sex, etc. Usually orgasms are accompanied by ejaculation in males. Ejaculation by females at the time of orgasm is a widely debated topic. The debate centers on whether ejaculation can occur in a woman.

If by ejaculation one means the expulsion of progenitive fluids at the time of orgasm, then females have not been shown to have that capability. However, if the word ejaculate is used in its basic sense—to eject or discharge abruptly, then some women have the ability to eject and/or discharge fluids during sex and at the time of orgasm. Often a woman will secrete an increased amount of vaginal fluids during climax and sometimes in a pulsatile fashion similar to male ejaculation. In the

female, this ejaculate is of variable quantity and is usually clear or milky white in appearance. Female ejaculate largely comes from paraurethral glands and ducts that are stimulated at the time of intercourse. This ejaculate will flow or squirt through the urethra and sometimes around it. Urine may be a component of this fluid to a greater or lesser degree.

The classic sexual response cycle has five successive phases: excitement, plateau, orgasm, resolution, and then refractory period. Orgasm is the central and high point of this cycle. Some orgasms occur spontaneously due to psychological stimulation, or as a result of unintentional friction or physical stimulation. Most orgasms, however, are brought about intentionally as a result of concentrated effort during sexual interplay using the hands, other body parts, or some device.

Multiple orgasms are an actuality. Women tend to be more capable of this phenomenon than men, but males are capable of successive orgasms also. Women have a relatively short refractory period following orgasm, or no refractory period at all. Women, therefore, can be brought to orgasm in a serial fashion more easily than men, if desire and circumstances permit.

The male refractory period is an event well known to sex partners, but not always well accepted and understood. It is normal for a man to have a refractory period following orgasm and especially orgasm with ejaculation. The refractory period in males is variable from individual to individual and with circumstance, and this period of sexual apathy and flagging response tends to get longer with advancing age. Concentrated, inventive stimulation can often coax a man out of refractory mode and back into sexual action. So, multiple orgasms in a short time span are a possibility for males but are not the norm. The quantity of male ejaculate tends to decrease and/or go away altogether with rapidly-occurring, serial orgasms.

Orgasms are characterized by intense physical and psychological pleasure. Involuntary muscular contractions occur at these times especially in the genitals, but may involve the whole body. The rhythmic contractions and spasms of an orgasm can go on for long periods, similar to the ebbing aftershocks of an earthquake. The outward expressions of an orgasm are individualistic and tend to mirror the innermost personality trait of the one who is climaxing, though not absolutely; i.e. introverted people may be more subdued during orgasms, and extroverted people may be more expressive. Even so, sexual partners may display one persona in public and a totally different personality in the privacy of the bedroom. The outward manifestations of an individual's orgasm tend to repeat themselves, generally speaking, every time that person climaxes; although one can learn to be more or less expressive. Outside of that, when you have experienced one orgasm, you have experienced one orgasm, and response character cannot be predicted.

A variety of vocalizations spontaneously occur during orgasm, but unfortunately many Christians report restraining these verbal expressions of pleasure. In the main, Christian women are thought to be more repressive of such vocalizations than Christian men. This reticence is thought to be a carryover from a time when believers were taught that sex had a purpose—procreation; and pleasure, though an ever-present side effect, was not to be embraced. Strait-laced, Bible-believing folks were to not show elation except during times of church celebrations, i.e. preaching and praise, it was taught, and women were expected to be even more decorous than men. The residue of such teaching has stifled expressions of pleasure that should be a natural part of orgasm. If ever there is a time when you should go with the flow and express yourself, it is at the time of orgasm.

Not all people can have orgasms, even though to do so is a normal, physiologic response. If your sexual apparatus and appetite are conducive to orgasms, then it is silly to not enjoy a climax when it occurs. Ideally, orgasms should occur during appropriate sexual intercourse between a man and his wife.

Though the following scriptures do not pinpoint the exact time of orgasm, or give step by step details of what led up to the climax, Songs of Solomon 4:16–5:1 gives good evidence of a receptive wife and the orgasmic pleasure derived by her husband from sexual intercourse. The speech is flowery, but one can hardly miss the message: "Awake, O north wind; and come, thou south; blow upon my garden that the spices thereof may flow out. Let my beloved come into his garden, and eat his pleasant fruits." If that passage is allegorical, as some theologians write, then it is allegory based upon one of the fieriest sexual utterances ever. Here we have a wife wishing that the scent of her vagina—an attractant aroma—would come to the nose of her husband, so that he might come and partake of what she is offering. Later in the fifth song, the husband exclaims: "I have come into my garden, my sister, my spouse: I have gathered my myrrh with my spice; I have eaten my honeycomb with my honey; I have drunk my wine with my milk" (verse one). In other words, he is saying, "That sex was thrilling and fulfilling to me!" Now it doesn't take making a quantum leap to assume that this husband had an orgasm and is now very, very satisfied.

Orgasms make the sex act highly appealing to assure our drive for procreation—that drive is to be carried out within the confines of marriage. Also, orgasms intensify the intimacy and bonding that occurs between sex partners at the times of climax. Humans (and some other species) are physically programmed to enjoy these sexual peaks, and can do little to prevent the pleasure short of medications and genital surgery.

Don't be ashamed or guilty for experiencing this God-given gift! Open up and express yourself verbally, musically, physically, acrobatically—however you want—during times of orgasm. Just don't hurt yourselves or frighten the neighbors. Be determined to enjoy these heightened sexual moments in the intimacy of your married bed and with the blessings of our Lord.

Summary Points:

- Orgasms invigorate the sexual experience and were designed by God to be pleasurable, to keep us coming back for more.
- Our tendency to seek the pleasure of an orgasm assures the procreation of the species and the marital bonding that God intended.
- Express your orgasms however you see fit, but don't fight or repress the feeling out of guilt or shame.

Discussion Questions:

- What is the effect of repeatedly repressing orgasmic expression?
- What (if anything) should be done if your spouse represses orgasmic expression?
- Must all instances of copulation end in orgasm?
- Is an orgasm necessary for sexual satisfaction during intercourse?
- There is no one path to orgasm. How should you lead your spouse to do things your way, sexually?
- Must an orgasm happen for pregnancy to take place?
- Is one being greedy or over-indulgent to try to have multiple orgasms during a single sexual encounter?

Isn't Foreplay Just Playing Around?

Well, certainly it can be! There is a lot of satisfaction to be gained from random sex play carried out for no other reason than a lighthearted mood—playing around. Married couples need not confine their sexual interplay to copulation only, nor must they focus on the sexual destination at the expense of the journey. There is so much more pleasure to be gained from investigating, lingering over, and savoring the fullness of your spouse's body during times of intimacy. However, most people participate in foreplay with a goal in mind—that of heightening the pleasure and receptiveness of their partner prior to some definitive sex act—often coitus. Even the word *foreplay* suggests temporary or mimicking behavior meant to precede the main act. You get to decide what the main act will be.

In the Songs of Solomon 4:5–6, the writer gives a classic example of foreplay: "Thy two breasts are like two young roes that are twins, which feed among the lilies. Until the day break, and the shadows flee away,

I will get me to the mountain of myrrh and the hill of frankincense."

This is an ornate description of a man who appreciates the beauty and attractiveness of his lover's body—most specifically her breasts; so much so that he plans to spend a great deal of time paying attention to those breasts, that to him are as aromatic and desirable as the precious perfumes *myrrh* and *frankincense*.

His plan is to linger on those uplifted parts of her anatomy even until dawn. Let your imagination figure out what he plans to do during and after his lingering. While no one can argue against the pleasures of coitus, foreplay broadens sexual exploration and excitation to areas including and beyond the genitalia. Done properly, this type stimulation can make coitus that much more satisfying.

The kinds of things that constitute foreplay are just as varied as the individuals who are participating in the stimulation. Everything from lightly blowing with the mouth to nipping with the teeth, to stroking with the toes, pressing against one another, and much, much more can be considered foreplay.

Many couples will use sex toys during foreplay. Sex toys are various gadgets used to enhance sexual pleasure. Oils, gels, jam and jelly, as well as sundry other sexual aids are similar to sex toys in terms of purpose. Such paraphernalia can be purchased, developed, or otherwise discovered by inquisitive couples. While there is nothing obviously sinful about using such enhancers, Christians must be careful to not become contraption-crazy and go overboard in a sticky haze of sexual delirium. Although sex is surely meant to be enjoyable, the Christians' quest should not be for the ultimate orgasm, as much as it should be for the ultimate walk with God.

Also, be careful when seeking or securing sex equipment. Often doing so will take you to Web sites and or stores where pornography is prevalent. Believers are encouraged to "abstain from all appearance of evil" (1 Thessalonians 5:22), and frequent trips to such venues can certainly appear suspect to others. Not only that, many Christians have stumbled and been lured away by the temptations that abound in such places. For this reason, Christian couples should seriously consider not patronizing such merchandisers. At a minimum, a husband and wife should try to be together when choosing these devices and/or visiting such places.

Here's another example from Songs of Solomon 7:8–10:

> Thy breasts shall be as clusters of the vine, and the smell of thy nose like apples; And the roof of thy mouth like the best wine, for my beloved, that goeth down sweetly, causing the lips of those that are sleep to speak. I am my beloved's, and his desire is toward me.

Here again we have the words of a husband who appreciates every aspect of his wife's body. He even thinks her nose looks and smells good and delights in it, along with her breasts, and her mouth. Nowhere yet has there been any mention of the vagina or of copulation. His plan is to enjoy her other physical assets first because she is sweet—goes down like a smooth wine and is fine enough to make a dead man talk (loose translation)!

While these examples are of a man appreciating his wife, the same admonition applies to a woman appreciating her husband. Foreplay works both ways. Do not assume your husband is always ready for sex and never in need of intentional stimulation. The wife who liberally puts in time romancing, caressing and touching during the sexual prelims, can usually expect a good return on her investment. The take-home message is that spouses should relax, take their time, and enjoy the sexual experience fully; that means using foreplay generously throughout the encounter.

While foreplay is a desirable and rewarding part of the sexual encounter, there are some practices that are outside the bounds of what is proper for Christians. Sadism, masochism and other behaviors aimed at physical and psychological harm fit into this category of unsavory and unacceptable routines.

Sadism and masochism are psychiatrically aberrant behaviors. These practices run counter to the idea of giving and receiving love, and are not appropriate behaviors for Christians. This is not to speak against reciprocated sexual interplay that may get a bit aggressive or rough during periods of intense passion, but of deliberate attempts to cause and or receive pain during the sex act. Some people enjoy stormy, tempestuous sex, and should feel free to follow their sexual mood, but sadism and masochism are psychiatric states that should be prayerfully avoided.

People who practice sadism get sexual gratification from being cruel, causing pain, and/or degrading another. By no stretch of the imagination are Christians to enjoy being cruel to one another. Proverbs 11:17, protests, "He that is cruel troubleth his own flesh," which is to say, cruelty breeds further disturbance within the psyche of the initiator as well as the psyche of the victim.

Masochism is the circumstance where sexual gratification is gained from pain, deprivation and degradation. Again, Christian principles call for us to lift one another and not beat one another down. Such behaviors cannot justifiably be part of the Christian ethic.

While the world counts such practices as forms of foreplay, Christians should not. Don't hurt one another sexually and don't ask to be sexually hurt. There's enough pain in this world without Christians deliberately bringing it into their bedrooms.

Kissing, rubbing, tweaking, licking, and stroking various erogenous zones are the more readily recognized forms of foreplay, but foreplay technique should only be limited by the imaginations of the persons involved. The wise sex partner learns that foreplay is as much emotional as it is physical. To that end, foreplay aficionados should not forget the visual, the verbal, the environment, or the mood. It has been said that *foreplay begins in the kitchen.* The message inherent in that quote is: letting your spouse know you care about and support them on non-sexual levels outside the bedroom will often yield high sexual dividends once the bedroom door is closed.

It is popularly believed that women are slow to arousal and require crescendo foreplay before being emotionally open to copulation. This requirement for progressive arousal is true of some women, but certainly not all. Indeed, recent sexual research has shown, generally speaking, that women are as quickly aroused as men. Where men and women actually differ is in what arouses them—when and under what circumstances they are enlivened. Foreplay will often help sexual partners learn one another's erotic desires, preferences, and triggers. Such information is invaluable to spouses who want to satisfy their partners as well as themselves.

And what if your spouse does require foreplay to become receptive to your advances? Don't fight against this need. Just as the earnest kneading of dough can yield warm, tasty bread, the patient kneading of the human body and spirit can yield a sexual bounty that is just as pleasing (if not more so) to your other appetites.

Again, the Bible doesn't specifically speak of foreplay but gives many examples of it. Look once more at the Songs of Solomon chapter seven. In the following passage from verse eight, the writer compares his love to a palm tree then goes on to declare, "I will go up to the palm tree, I will take hold of the boughs thereof."

This passage naturally and figuratively describes foreplay at its purest and best. Your job is to take hold of your lover's body in ways your lover wants to be touched, held, and embraced. You also are to take hold of the character and tenor of your love-making. Focus on giving pleasure and satisfaction to your mate. When you do that, usually the effort is reciprocated. Just remember, the same things you do prior to the initiation of coitus often can be carried on once you have started and when you are done. So, the optimal sequence for your sexual encounter should be *foreplay*, then *your mainstay*, followed by *after-play*. If you're blessed, there might be an instant *replay*. Assuredly, if you have taken hold of these matters correctly, you won't be just playing around.

Summary Points:

- There are unacceptable forms of foreplay such as sadism and masochism.
- The goal of foreplay should be to increase sexual pleasure, not to injure another physically or psychologically.
- Most spouses appreciate foreplay prior to copulation.
- Foreplay adds to the bonding that occurs between spouses during sexual intimacy.
- The type of foreplay couples practice is individualistic, so discuss and explore to find what is right for you.
- Sex toys are acceptable for use in a marriage relationship; pornography is not. Be careful when you explore the former and don't explore the latter at all.

Discussion Questions:

- What is the boundary between rough sex and sadism or masochism?
- How important is play outside the bedroom to play that occurs once the bedroom door has been closed?
- What should be the guiding principle for foreplay between a wife and husband?

- Should foreplay be a requirement before coitus takes place?
- What areas of the body should be excluded from foreplay?
- What are your thoughts about sex toys and other sexual aids?

Should I Tell It Like It Is?

In Songs of Solomon 5:2–4, the writer dramatizes the power of the spoken word: "It is the voice of my beloved that knocketh, saying, open to me my sister, my love, my dove, my undefiled...and my bowels were moved for him." This is powerful imagery describing a husband coming to his wife's bed chamber. His words as he approaches are a strong stimulant that causes sensual rumblings deep inside his spouse. The movement of bowels is not as we think today, for in ancient times the bowels were thought to be above the diaphragm—an area of vital organs, including the heart. This verse might well be interpreted, *my heart leaped for him*! Such words as those in verse two are even more powerful when uttered in anticipation of sexual interplay. The wife is being called upon to *open* not only the door of her bed chamber but the door of her love chamber.

God expects us to use as many senses as we can during sexual encounters with our spouses. Our ability to speak gives great expression to those senses and is highly useful and stimulating during sexual interplay. Tell your sexual partner what you're feeling, tasting, smelling, hearing, and seeing. Your lover shouldn't have to guess about where you are in the sexual intercourse process, but should be given regular verbal clues. Sure, moans, groans, and body language are exciting hints given during sex, but a bit of direct verbal communication can take the experience to new levels.

Most individuals have sexual fantasies, preferences, and desires, and each knows when those fantasies are being fulfilled. There would be much more mutual sexual satisfaction if partners talked more and gave positive feedback to their lovers. If you have gone so far as to commit your body and sexual spirit to another person, why would you not also commit to satisfying that person as much as you possibly can, and in return, being satisfied. Tell it like it is! Tell your lover what you want, when you want to have it, and how you want it delivered. Your spouse should not have to play a game of figure-out-what-I-like during your sexual encounters. Unless you and your lover specifically get off on that sort of mystery-detective sex play, abandon it altogether. Actually, it is a great waste of time and sexual energy for two individuals to be married, sexually and socially intimate, but unwilling to share with one another their sexual preferences and wishes. Too many couples have spent too many years together, sexually unfulfilled, because they wouldn't talk about what they expect from their mate in the bedroom.

Tell your partner what you want sexually, and be as explicit as possible. Better yet, help your spouse discover your preferences. There are few things more physically stimulating than a dedicated time of loving, ardent, sexual exploration. If you lack knowledge and experience, but still want to explore new sexual scenarios for your marriage, there are manuals, photos, and descriptions that can be purchased at bookstores to guide these intimate investigations. If need be, set aside special times to discover your sexual likes and dislikes, open your mind to new possibilities, and don't forget to use all your senses.

Different folks, different strokes is really true in this sensual arena. Some people are genuinely turned on by certain smells. Those smells have a stimulant quality for such people and heighten libido, driving them on to the peak of excitement. For others, certain sounds during sex are a turn on and bring them to special levels of arousal. Almost all people enjoy being touched in certain ways in special places, but just as many are turned off by touch in the wrong way, at the wrong time, or on the wrong area of the body. Our spouses should know these likes and dislikes. We're all very individualistic in our preferences, and the things that have an aphrodisiac quality for one, may do nothing at all for another. The bottom line is that we should not be wasting our sexual time together trying to figure out what the other wants (unless, of course, that's your thing).

Here are just a few words on the topic of dirty, sex talk:

Many Christians are not very good at this type lingo anymore (if they ever were). After coming over to the Lord's side and immersing themselves in his word, it often becomes counter-intuitive and difficult to use explicitly vulgar, highly sex-charged words in everyday speech and even in the throes of passion. This topic is further complicated by the individual perspectives we bring to the sexual encounter. What may be considered gross and rude talk to one person may be welcoming and sexually stimulating conversation to another.

Scriptures give numerous instructions about how our everyday speech should be, but little instruction about our bedroom-speak. Following are two Bible passages that tell about the kind of speech Christians should avoid:

> But now ye also put off all these; anger, wrath, malice, blasphemy, filthy communication out of your mouth.
> (Colossians 3:8)

> Not that which goeth into the mouth defileth a man; but that which cometh out of the mouth, this defileth a man.
> (Matthew 15:11)

These and other similar verses point to the kind of communication that should occur between individuals during their regular, daily activities; they suggest a mindset that is Christian and a way of expressing oneself that is indicative of that state of mind. These scriptures are not specifically aimed at bedroom talk, however.

If somewhere deep in your psyche there is the need to whisper, chant, or even shout explicitly erotic terms in order to accentuate your sexual pleasure, then there's nothing to stop you short of your own conscience and vocabulary. Other than that, make sure the doors and windows are closed and locked and that nobody else can hear or interrupt you and yours during your verbal, erotic eruptions.

This final statement almost goes without saying: When your spouse takes the step of opening up and telling you what he or she wants sexually, then you should do your best to deliver, or you're in for a lot of anguish and long discussions about why you are not taking care of the business at hand. Loving, honest communication is one of the most important aspects of the marital relationship—no less so in the bedroom. As mentioned in an earlier chapter, this kind of communication should begin during the dating period to lessen the likelihood of surprises and disappointments after marriage. This is conversation for two people who are deeply committed to one another. That being said, you should not surrender your principles or your conscience for the sake of the sexual relationship. If your partner is asking for and expects you to perform sexual acts that are unacceptable to you, then let your difference of opinion be known as gently as possible. Next, try the request against the Word to see if you're on solid spiritual grounds. Remember that your spouse is due sexual gratification—from you. When necessary, use godly advice and advisors to help find solutions and compromise. Above all else be true to yourself and true to God as you relate to your spouse.

Summary Points:

- It is okay to speak up and tell your spouse what you are feeling during sexual intercourse.
- It is just as acceptable to tell your spouse what you specifically want done or not done during sexual intercourse.

- When your spouse has told you what he or she wants during sexual intercourse, go to great lengths to fulfill the request if it is at all within your sensibilities.
- Sexual fantasies can become problematic especially when they get into the realm of the criminal, illegal, pornographic, lustful or the psychologically aberrant.

Discussion Questions:

- Try this exercise: With your spouse, write down five acceptable words and five unacceptable words spoken during sexual encounters; discuss them.
- What factors prevent partners from talking about sex, during sex?
- Do you want your spouse to know your sexual fantasies; sexual *turn ons* and *turn offs*? Care to explain?
- Would you rather tell your spouse what you want sexually or have your mate figure it out?
- During sex, what's the benefit of knowing what your spouse is feeling and thinking? What's the down side?
- Can we control our sexual fantasies?

Is Sex During Menses Sinful?

The Bible is very specific about coitus during the time of menses; it forthrightly teaches us to not have sex—copulation at that time. Leviticus 15:19–20 reads:

> And if a woman have an issue, and her issue in her flesh be blood, she shall be put apart seven days: and whosoever toucheth her shall be unclean until the even. And every thing that she lieth upon in her separation shall be unclean: every thing also that she sitteth upon shall be unclean.

Leviticus 18:19 reads: "Also thou shalt not approach unto a woman to uncover her nakedness, as long as she is put apart for her uncleanness." Leviticus 20:18 adds: "And if a man shall lie with a woman having her sickness, and shall uncover her nakedness; he hath discovered her fountain, and she hath uncovered the fountain of her blood: and both of them shall be cut off from among their people." These scriptures describe menses as a time of *uncleanness* and *sickness*. Biblical patriarchs,

although not having modern medical research to inform their decisions, recognized intuitively the altered cultural and physical conditions present during the time of menstruation, and they forbade copulation and most other forms of sexual contact. The prohibition against menstrual sex from Old Testament times has been carried forward to today's church, and is evident in unchurched society as well.

Numerous printed accounts, mostly historical and sociological, tell of women being ostracized and physically banished during the time of their monthly period. In truth, the menstrual houses and huts of the past were often places of sexual rendezvous in addition to sexual seclusion.

Menstruation is physically characterized by the discharge of blood, secretions, and tissue debris from the vagina, classically every twenty-eight days for a period of seven days. There is a physiologic purpose behind this flow of blood and there are numerous physiologically induced changes that happen to a woman at that time. During a woman's period, the uterine membrane is thinned, pelvic vessels are engorged, and the pH of the vagina becomes more alkaline. These physical changes make the vaginal and urinary apparatus slightly more susceptible to bacterial infection than at other times. The male urethra and nearby prostate also are more susceptible to infections if copulation takes place during menstruation due to the piston effect that is part of the thrusting of coitus; this thrusting motion forces bacteria-rich fluids upwards into the male's otherwise closed urethral system. In addition, bacteria are more likely to thrive during a woman's period because of increased moisture and the compressing effect caused by vaginal pads or tampons. Copulation during these times stirs up the increased bacteria and has been shown to raise the likelihood of urinary tract infections in women especially, and men to a much lesser degree.

During menses, the alkaline nature of the vagina, the vaginal effluent, and the bacterial environment made up mostly of E. coli from the anus, come together to form a distinct odor, which many find unpleasant. Various compounds and perfumes have been developed to mask this menstrual odor. Even so, for cultural, aesthetic, and reasons of personal preference, many men back away from vaginal intercourse during menses.

Still, there are men who are not at all sexually deterred by a woman's period, and those who find the distinct menstrual odor particularly stimulating (it acts as a pheromone). For such men, sexual urgings are heightened during menstruation. Also, there are a plethora of women who see menstruation as neither a physical nor psychological barrier to sexual interplay. For many such women, the hormonal changes that accompany their monthly periods turn them on sexually rather than turn them off. Consequently, some Christians are faced with a dilemma. The Bible declares, "Thou shalt not approach" (Leviticus 18:19); their minds and urgings say approach, and the only thing standing in the way is a bit of inconvenience.

In any seemingly uncertain ethical situation like this, Christians should follow the Bible's teaching. That's a good rule of thumb when Bible believers are faced with a decision of principle and are not sure about how to proceed. Don't follow only what you think; be careful about following what the world thinks, or what science believes, but follow the Bible and the whole of what it has to say on the subject. The Bible is the Christian's guidebook. On the matter of copulation during menses, the Bible is very specific and unequivocal, so the answer to this chapter's question is, "No, don't do it; don't have copulatory sex during menses; show restraint instead!"

It is worthwhile here to discuss the concept of *discipline*, one definition of which is *to bring to a state of order and obedience by control.* A Christian's obedience should be to God and his Word. Order and control is what comes to our lives when we submit to and obey biblical teachings. The Bible calls us to a life of discipline and also expects us to do things "decently and in order" (1 Corinthians 14:40). In truth, we cannot be good followers of Christ without having discipline in our lives.

Some Christian practices are carried out not so much for their feel good effect, their rationality, or because they are universally popular, but because Scripture teaches it, and we discipline ourselves to do what Scripture says. We may not be happy with the way the Bible has directed us in all cases, but if we are patient, old folks tell, "We'll understand it better by and by." What our Christian ancestors meant is that in time and with deeper spiritual maturity scriptural directives often become clearer. Many actions fall under this discipline principle and sex during menses is but one of them.

While sex is good, it must not be the underlying purpose of our existence. We must not be consumed with sexual thoughts all the time. The Bible teaches that all of us are prone to inappropriate thoughts and actions (some more than others)—"For out of the heart proceed evil thoughts" (Matthew 15:19). With God's help, we can train ourselves to bring thoughts and actions under control. A well-suited scripture from the book of Philippians directs:

> Whatsoever things are true, whatsoever things are honest, whatsoever things are just, whatsoever things are poor, whatsoever things are lovely, whatsoever things are of good report; if there be any virtue, and if there be any praise, think on these things.
>
> (Philippians 4:8)

We must not pursue sex at any cost and in any setting. Congregational or other spiritual gatherings are examples of times and places where we should discipline ourselves to shut out the sexual and concentrate on the spiritual. A Christian's ultimate goal in life should be to have a deeper relationship with our Lord and Savior Jesus Christ, best achieved through increased time in study and prayer.

Why not think of the time you spend refraining from sex during menses as a kind of sexual sabbath (a period of rest)? A sabbath is a good thing on many levels, and a sexual respite is no different. So, during your hiatus from vaginal sex around the time of menses, devote yourself to other pursuits, including prayer, fasting and the reading of God's Word.

Menstruating women are not unclean in the sense of being overall germ-ridden and unhealthy, although certain parts of the anatomy are bacteria-rich. In the Bible, women going through their period were described as unclean to accentuate the prohibition against copulation during that time and the cultural abhorrence attached to anyone with an issue of blood.

These explanations notwithstanding, wives should be willing to stimulate their sexually aroused husbands in other ways when menstruation is present. Also, husbands at this time of the month should seek to pleasure their wives in ways other than vaginal involvement (if wives want this kind of contact). Such loving stimulation will lessen the pangs of coital abstinence and bring more variety to your overall sexual scheme.

Summary Points:

* Sexual intercourse — copulation — during menses is not sanctioned by the Bible.
* Plan to take a *sexual sabbath* during times of menses and spend extra time in prayer and dedication to the Lord.
* If you cannot keep your sexual urges under control during menses, then with your spouse, look for other ways besides copulation to obtain release.

Discussion Questions:

* When the Bible describes a woman as being *unclean* during the time of menses, is that a literal description? Explain your answer.
* In today's world, should menstruating women be kept apart from the general public?
* Should a *sexual sabbath* encompass more than what is described in the chapter above?

- Some people recommend sex during and/or immediately following menses for a contraceptive reason. Explain that reason?
- Sexual discipline extends beyond *sex during menses*. Give some other examples where sexual discipline is needed?

Are You Keeping It Clean?

Do you recall as a child sometimes coming to the dinner table without washing your hands, or trying to sneak off to school without washing your ears? If your mother caught you being negligent in these things, she might very well tell you, "Get in there and wash yourself!" If truth be told, and depending on the mother, she might add a pet name and a few other choice words to the command. A similar instruction is given here regarding sexual matters—the same one a mother might give: "Get in there and wash yourself!"

Let's be honest, there are individuals who are sexually turned on by pungent body smells and grubby environments; they are not in the majority. If you have yourself one of those type spouses, then skip this chapter. Otherwise, in preparation for most forms of sexual intercourse, "Get in there and wash yourself!"

The male and female genitalia, while attractive on many levels, can harbor any number of germs, rashes, unpleasant surprises, and odors. These body parts are usually hidden away for propriety's sake, and the hiding places and garments make for dark, warm, sometimes moist areas—a ready culture medium for the growth of organisms. Such areas must be cleaned regularly. Sexually transmitted infections will be discussed in more detail in a later chapter, but there are medical conditions that can be transmitted from sex partner to partner, often the result of poor hygiene. This list of diseases includes (in part) vaginitis, urethritis, Candida, urinary tract infections, lice, and scabies.

Most sexual partners are operating under the assumption that their mate participates in some form of daily hygiene ritual; and that these rituals include close attention to, and cleansing of body orifices. Most spouses find it difficult to tell their mates about offensive breath or malodorous underarms. They cringe at having to remind their lover to bathe and wash with special attention to skin folds and privy parts. A spouse who won't tell you about your lack of hygiene will usually show it by being less than open to your sexual advances. Don't put your partner through such anguish. Consider a playful shower or bath as a form of foreplay before lovemaking. However, serious body cleansing should be done with diligent effort, a good soap, and no company except maybe someone to come in to scrub your back and then leave.

You might want to discuss with your spouse the use of deodorants, perfumes, gels, and other scented, tasty products that make the sex act more enjoyable (for some people). Some folks like their sex basic; some want their sex sugary sweet; still others want a bit of spice with their erotic escapades. But before you spray or rub anything on your body, wash that body often and well.

Cleanliness really is next to godliness in sexual matters. The Bible gives no specific direction on washing oneself for the purpose of sexual intercourse. However, numerous verses in Songs of Solomon describe how your lover's body can tantalize the senses. Chapter one, verses two and three: "Let him kiss me with the kisses of his mouth: for thy love is better than wine. Because of the savour of thy good ointments, thy name is as ointment poured forth." See also verses thirteen and fourteen in that same chapter: "A bundle of myrrh is my wellbeloved unto me; he shall lie all night betwixt my breasts. My beloved is unto me like a cluster of camphire in the vineyards of Engedi." While these verses give no instructions in washing, they do emphasize the importance of the senses—especially the senses of smell and taste—to the lovemaking process.

Certain smells have a pheromonal quality. A pheromone is any chemical substance or smell released or emitted by a species that serves to influence the physiology or behavior of members of the same species, often functioning as an attractant to the opposite sex. While pheromones have been well-documented in animals and insects, to date, no true pheromone receptor has been identified in humans. A defined receptor notwithstanding, most researchers believe humans react to stimulants emitted by other humans, just as insects and other animals react. According to many who have researched pheromones in humans, the nose is the receptor—pure and simple. Studies have shown that the sweat of humans takes on an odor following puberty, and this sweaty smell is thought to be a stimulant to the opposite sex. Anecdotal evidence seems to support this sweaty belief, even if science has not found the exact answer to the pheromone receptor question.

There was a controlled experiment done approximately ten years ago that showed the menstrual cycles of a group of women living in the same sorority house becoming synchronous. The natural adjustment in the periods of the women was thought to be mediated by pheromones. This experiment gave additional validity to the existence of such secreted substances.

Most people believe that during sexual encounters, certain smells are either a *turn on* or a *turn off*. Except for those individuals who lean toward giving off and experiencing musty, pungent odors, most others prefer neutral or aromatic smells, best achieved after first cleansing the body well. Also, good hygiene is conducive to good health. Regular washing and cleansing will keep unfavorable organisms from setting up shop in various parts of your system, causing dis-ease. The healthier you are, the happier you are; and the happier you are, the healthier your sex life will be. On so many different levels, God wants us to keep our sex lives clean.

Summary Points:

- All areas of the body, especially the privy parts, should be washed regularly.
- Most spouses prefer their partners' bodies to be clean and good-smelling during sexual intercourse.

- The sense of smell can accentuate the pleasure of sexual encounters; don't underestimate its importance.
- It is never too late to give hygiene tips to your spouse, but they should be given tactfully and lovingly.
- Make a list of smells that are pleasing to you; a list of smells that are not. Now make a list of smells that are sexually arousing to you. Share these lists with your spouse.

Discussion Questions:

- Do you believe in human pheromones? If so, are they at play in everyday life even when sexual intercourse is not occurring?
- What's the origin of the phrase *cleanliness is next to Godliness*?

Sexual
Troubles

Can
I Just
Look?

> For all that is in the world, the lust of the flesh, and
> the lust of the eyes, and the pride of life, is not of the
> Father, but is of the world. And the world passeth
> away, and the lust thereof: but he that doeth the will
> of God abideth forever.
>
> 1 John 2:16–17

This scripture helps answer the question, "Can I just
look?" We can look if we don't allow our looking to
become lustful, and we are least likely to become lustful
if we limit our lingering looks to our own spouse.

Voyeurism is the practice of obtaining sexual gratification by looking at sexual objects or acts, especially
secretively—the *Peeping Tom* syndrome. Numerous
voyeurs have been in the news in recent years, especially with the advent of miniature cameras and video
devices. Voyeurism is not a proper practice for Christians, although believers should be permitted to look at
their spouses longingly whenever the mood hits them.
While any spouse may sporadically glance at their mate

during regular activities at home or out in the public, spouses should not be relegated to glances and the occasional peek, but should be given full viewing rights and privileges. Full viewing rights and privileges do not necessarily include looking at your spouse while they are engaged in the privy functions of daily living, or otherwise seeking private time. So, whether you can *just look* depends on what you're looking at and the circumstances under which you are looking.

Within marriages, spouses are often reluctant to display their bodies because of negative body images or the privacy rules taught during childhood. Parents were correct to teach that genitalia and other privy parts should be covered in public. This cover-up edict, however, was not meant to carry over to marriage during times of sexual interplay. When we are involved in sexual intercourse, openness and exposure should be the rule—if that's what turns you on. By the same token, if you and your spouse like to keep everything under wraps, then that's all right too. You may not want to strut your stuff, but hopefully, in front of your spouse, you won't hide it, either.

Your mate often finds you much more attractive than you think. Many individuals have emotions that are triggered by the visual image, and your spouse may be one such person. If you're denying your mate the view of your body in its entire and most particular splendor, then you are probably limiting the level of pleasure the two of you can achieve during times of passionate sharing. Usually your spouse will let you know in some way when he or she wants to *just look*. Be open to such cues; unwrap and give this gift willingly—it tends to be a gift that helps the two of you keep on giving and giving again sexually.

Unfortunately, in this age of easily available media and cyberspace, the practice of looking causes many Christians to get caught up in the snare of pornography—its reading and viewing. Pornography is a realm where Christians should not *just look*. While courts, sexologists, and sociologists have argued the definition of pornography, the masses seem to agree that the term describes sexually explicit, obscene writings, photos, movies, videos, or other material that is intended to sexually arouse. Most arguments, when they occur, revolve around when and whether such erotic offerings move from the benignly risqué to the blatantly reprehensible. At any rate, pornographic viewing is a lustful behavior, and the Bible calls us away from this type preoccupation.

Christian women and men often feel guilty when they see someone of the opposite sex (not their spouse) and find that person attractive; often they equate having looked and seen to having sinned. Such thoughts represent guilt unfounded. Unless you are prepared to go through life blindfolded, you will from time to time see someone or something that trips your sexual triggers. For these type situations, the question is not so much whether you looked, as it is whether you *just* looked and then looked away—naturally and mentally. Did you stare? Did you fixate on the attractive person? Did you allow your thoughts to be carried away to lustful musings about the individual and/or the situation? Jesus said in Matthew 5:28 "that whosoever looketh on a woman to lust after her hath committed adultery with her already in his heart."

When someone other than your spouse stimulates your sexual imagination, you should detach from that person and circumstance as quickly as possible. Think about something else. Go somewhere else. Exercise vigorously. Take a cold shower. Pray earnestly. Whatever legal involvement successfully moves your mind away from the sexual temptation in front of you that is the tactic you should use.

The classic biblical illustration of someone doing more than *just* looking, is the story of David and his involvement with Bathsheba—Second Samuel chapter eleven. In this example, Bible scholars have pointed out the apparent idleness of David, because he was at home "at the time when kings go forth to battle" (verse ten); the message being—idle minds are the devil's workshops, and Christians should be more earnestly engaged in the work of the Lord leaving little time for aimless, meandering thoughts.

It is difficult to find fault with David walking upon the roof of his house and inadvertently seeing Bathsheba bathing: "And it came to pass in the eveningtide, that David arose from off his bed, and walked upon the roof of the king's house: and from the roof he saw a woman washing herself; and the woman was very beautiful to look upon" (verse two). Some theologians believe David's rooftop walk was not inadvertent but intentional because he knew the woman's bathing habits. Nonetheless, most analyzers of these scriptures see David's discovery of the nude, bathing woman as unintentional. Instead, most commentators point to David's response to Bathsheba as his undoing—"And David sent and inquired after the woman" (verse three). David later did more than just inquire, but initiated a sexual liaison, and the rest of the story is well-known biblical history. The sin exemplified here is not having looked, or having seen, but in lingering on what was seen and then following up with inappropriate action.

Make it a habit to quickly look away when you see something that is sexually explicit or inviting (and it is not being displayed by your spouse). When you linger over extraneous sexual images, that's when you get into the area of lust, and lust should be actively avoided by a Christian.

Sex is attractive, enticing, and a natural force that, among other things, assures the preservation of the human race. Society uses this sexual force to capture our attentions through advertisements, TV stories, and publications, etc. We are led down different pathways by the media for various forms of personal gain. This is a literal war for our bodies, our minds, and our souls. Scripture tells that God wants each of us "to know how to possess his vessel in sanctification and honour" (1 Thessalonians 4:4). The word *vessel* in this instance equates to body. We are to keep our bodies—our sexual ardor and emotions—under subjection and sanctified to God.

When considering the lessons learned from the story of David and Bathsheba, please also remember the "Joseph Principle" gleaned from Genesis 39:12. You may recall this as the story of Potiphar's wife and her attempt to seduce Joseph. That scripture explains: "And she caught him by his garment, saying, Lie with me:

and he left his garment in her hand, and fled, and got him out." To wit, when sexual impropriety has grabbed you and is trying to take over your mind, body, and soul, run, run away! Literally, run away!

So, you can *just look* all you want and all you are permitted within your own domain. Use your sense of sight to enjoy all the sensual gifts your spouse has to offer, and keep your eyes on your prize and not that of another.

Summary Points:

- It is okay for spouses to want to see one another's bodies and to show those bodies in their private moments together.
- When the sight or thought of your spouse is sexually stimulating, that is not a form of lust.
- When someone other than your spouse stirs your sexual imagination, quickly *look away, turn away,* and *run away* if need be.

Discussion Questions:

- What are the parts of the body that should be covered in public?
- Do we all have the same erogenous parts? Erogenous zones?
- What tactics can you use to prevent looking and being turned on by someone who is not your spouse?
- If you have to use the "Joseph Principle," you're already caught up in a sexual situation.

How do you prevent being caught up in the first place?

- How would you explain to your spouse that you don't want to see some particular part of their anatomy, or that you don't want a part of yours to be seen?
- Is it fair that you want to keep parts of your body out of sight?
- Do some people obtain sexual gratification from looking at the human body only? If so, is that an acceptable circumstance for a Christian?

Whatever Turns Us On, Right?

Wrong! Christian spouses sometimes turn on by viewing, reading, or listening to explicitly sexual material as a way of stimulating or accentuating their sex lives; such material is classified as pornography.

The word pornography is of Greek origin. *Porne* means prostitute and *graphia* means to write or record. Literally, the word suggests the writing and/or recording of matters regarding prostitutes. Pornography is defined as obscene writings, drawings, photographs, videos, and the like, especially those having little or no artistic merit and intended primarily to stimulate sexual desire. Porn is thought to be purveyed through some form of media, so live sex shows and lewd stories or jokes do not technically fit the definition. Even so, live sex shows and raunchy, sex-laden rhetoric and lyrics also should not be a form of Christian amusement, because such things promote a lascivious state of mind.

Pornography has been around as long as humans have been able to draw on the ground or write on stone tablets and the walls of structures. It is a multi-billion dollar industry that is pervasive to world culture and is growing with each passing year.

A great deal of the technological development of the Internet, the printing and photographic industry, is spurred on by the world's desire for pornographic media. The amount of time and money spent on this material is testimony to its pervasiveness in our society. Salman Rushdie, a well-known Indian-British writer, in his pornography-favoring essay *The East Is Blue*, wrote the following: "A free society should be judged by its willingness to accept porn." His words give only one side of the controversy that exists over the viewing of salacious materials by various world civilizations. Contrary to Rushdie's thinking is the belief that a Christian society is characterized by its determination to reject porn and all things related.

So far the United States has taken a public stance against pornography (even though there is widespread tolerance of its practice). So, while the practice is illegal and opposed by many segments of our society, it is as popular today as at any time in our country's existence. Scholars argue over whether porn benefits our society by giving an outlet for our sexual longings, or whether it hurts us by desensitizing us to lewd behavior and fueling our tendencies to act out that behavior among and against unwilling members of the public.

Pornographic media comes in two major forms— soft-core porn that does not involve vaginal penetration, and hardcore porn that surely does. Couples access porn together or individually as part of their sexual repertoire, and many use the viewing of porn as a form of foreplay before participating in sexual intercourse. Such couples believe porn fuels the imagination and literally *gets the juices flowing*—all toward a more vital sexual experience.

The viewing of porn can be an end in itself, however, and legions regularly access videos, DVDs, TV programs, adult peep shows and a plethora of Web sites to satisfy their lust for erotica. When Christians are away from home, temporarily staying in hotels and motels, they are confronted by readily available pornographic materials, available at low cost or free of charge and in the privacy of their rented rooms. These can be challenging situations for travelers. And when such temptation gets the best of you, unplug the TV, leave the room, and find some healthy distraction until you can gather your self-control.

Pornographic materials should not be part of a Christian's sex life, whether that person is married or not. Single Christians should do all within their power to keep themselves chaste and free from lustful viewing or reading habits, praying earnestly for God's help. When married couples permit themselves to be turned on by viewing porn, they break the sanctity of their one-on-one union by figuratively inviting others into what should be private sexual intercourse. There is nothing piously affirming about porn in the life of a Christian.

Christian couples must endeavor to find and cultivate sexual motivation within their own relationships and not through the explicit sexual exploits of others. When couples rely on the sexual actions of others to turn on their passions, they are actually participating in a form of psychological *group* or *pseudo-sex*.

It is very easy to be sensually carried away by the sight of the human body naked, or otherwise erotically posed and engaged, and then to become addicted to viewing such scenes. How-to sex manuals, photographs, and other media designed to inform and instruct should be an exception to this rule, but such learning should be done with caution. Most of us know when we're viewing material for the purpose of lusting rather than learning; and we must not fall victim to this enthralling but sinful temptation known as pornography.

The Matthew 5:28 verse mentioned earlier speaks of a man looking at a woman, the same principle holds true if a woman is looking at a man. The message here is that the lusts of the eyes can lead to sinful thoughts and actions thereby hindering our spiritual growth and maturity. When we view pornographic materials, we become fixated on the flesh—the look of it, the sensual workings of it, the sexual attraction of it. Pornography takes us far away from our godly natures and closer to our baser, human natures; and God wants us to do just the opposite.

First John 2:16 reminds us: "For all that is in the world, the lust of the flesh, and the lust of the eyes, and the pride of life, is not of the Father, but is of the world." Christian couples are called upon to bring flesh under submission and to seek sexual pleasure and titillation within their own unions and not from the abundance of erotica that bombards our senses.

Viewing pornography is an all-consuming habit for some, and an occasional pastime for others; either circumstance is an undesirable one for a Christian. Even though sex is a wonderful gift from God, he does not want our lives to be dominated by this most basic urge. Again, the disciplining of the flesh is to be a hallmark of the Christian's walk with God.

At one time, all people were slaves to their natural urges: "We all had our conversation in times past in the lusts of our flesh, fulfilling the desires of the flesh and of the mind" (Ephesians 2:3). Once saved, however, God wants his followers' attentions focused mainly on his deity and the development of a close relationship with him; after that, we are to love and serve those around us.

Christians, therefore, must fight against the lure of pornography. The powerful sexual feelings that porn engenders are born of very natural leanings. These feelings come out of that innate sex drive given us by our Creator. However, the sex urge was given to attract and bond us to one another in marriage unions and not for wanton entertainment.

Under normal circumstances, the sex drive does not leave us, and we will never be able to control and properly channel it without help from God. It is only through yielding our hearts, minds, and souls to the Master that we will develop spiritual discipline to help us turn a blind eye and a deaf ear to the potent enticement of pornography. Let's be determined that *whatever turns us on* will be something that is *right* in the sight of God!

Summary Points:

- Pornography should not be counted among the pastimes of Christians—married or single.
- Pornography is not an appropriate stimulant even in the privacy of our own bedrooms or hotel rooms.
- The viewing of pornography with your spouse is not acceptable; it is like inviting others into your sex play.
- When we come across media that is pornographic in nature, we should *look away, turn away*, and *run away* if need be.

Discussion Questions:

- If you're clicking through the TV channels with your remote control and come across something sexually titillating, how should you handle that situation?
- What should be done about unsolicited, letters, sexual emails and pop-up messages that appear on your computer at work? At home? What should you do with pornographic postal mail?
- What type materials would you consider sexually instructive, but not pornographic or sexually addictive?
- What is it about pornography that captures our attention and keeps us coming back for more? How do we effectively fight this temptation?

- What's the harm if a Christian, married couple views an erotic movie just to *get in the mood*?
- Is it acceptable for Christian couples to create their own sex videos featuring just the two of them?
- As we educate ourselves about pornography should we also more thoroughly legislate the practice?
- How do you personally determine what is pornographic in nature?
- Do most movies today have pornographic scenes? Explain.

Do Christians Spread STIs?

Yes, they do, depending on whom they are, their sexual history, and their current sexual habits. While our minds have been transformed and our spirits washed clean, our natural bodies are still vulnerable to the ills of this world, especially where we have been less than circumspect in our erotic behaviors. Promiscuous sexual behaviors from our pasts are known to cause ailments that can significantly impact our present and future lives—certain forms of cancer, AIDS, infertility, neonatal transmitted infections, and sexually transmitted infections (STIs).

The World Health Organization estimates that one million people daily are newly impacted by STIs. The STIs most common in the U.S. are Chlamydia, Gonorrhea, Trichomoniasis, Syphilis, Herpes, AIDS, Hepatitis, Genital Warts, Chancroid, Lice, and Scabies. All these are regularly transmitted during unprotected, sexual intercourse (the latter two even when standard forms of protection are used). Recent governmental reports regarding STIs show Chlamydia cases at a record high. Syphilis cases have risen, while Gonorrhea cases have remained about the same as last year. Chlamydia remains a particularly troublesome infection because it is often symptomless, so people can be carriers of the disease without even knowing it.

Most sexually active individuals in this country are familiar with the names of these sexually transmitted infections, but unevenly discuss them and fail to educate themselves about methods of transmission, symptoms, and prevention. Information about STIs is readily available to the public through health clinics, hospitals, physicians, and the Internet. And while use of barrier methods of protection during sexual intercourse is more popular today than in years past, so many people still have sex without protection and continue the incessant spread of these diseases.

The Bible suggests in Romans 1:27 that at times we will receive in our bodies "that recompense" of our errors and indiscretions. While this scripture is often tied directly to the practice of male homosexuality, its principle holds for illicit sex of any kind by any people, and for numerous other reckless, non-sexual actions. Paul's writing here to the church at Rome is consistent with another well recognized and accepted rule he gave to the Galatians: "Be not deceived; God is not mocked: for whatsoever a man soweth, that shall he also reap" (Galatians 6:7).

Earlier in this book, illicit sexual encounters were defined as *fornication*. Yet another scripture deals with this concept of fornication and the recompense that follows: "Flee fornication. Every sin that a man doeth is without the body; but he that committeth fornication sinneth against his own body" (1 Corinthians 6:18). Paul suggests here that sin in general has a negative effect on our mind and moves us further away from close relationship with God, but fornication does more. Fornication causes harm to the natural body as well, weakening our physical constitution and exposing us to various forms of disease.

Some Christians come to married sexual intercourse truly virginal, having not participated in coitus or any other intimate form of sexual interplay; these individuals, unfortunately, are a rare minority. Sexual virgins are not susceptible to sexually transmitted infections because they have avoided the mode of transmission—sex. However, for the sexual slate to truly be clean, both partners must come to the marriage bed having never had sexual intercourse or sexual encounters known to spread infection. This kind of sexually pure union is unusual in today's world. When such a union happens and both spouses remain sexually faithful to one another, then both partners can be free of worry about STIs. When such a union is not the case (the majority of the time), STIs are always a possibility. Christians, therefore, because of their pasts, may come to a legitimate sexual union unaware of pathogens they carry in their bodies. Also, extramarital sexual indiscretions, long forgiven, may leave behind pathologic traces that taint present relationships, no matter how exclusive those relationships are.

Christians must not assume their potential or current partners are educated about these diseases and must make learning about STIs a normal part of courtship and premarital preparation. Church leaders must assure such education for all Christians of appropriate age—married and unmarried.

In a sexual world replete with these deadly, life-altering illnesses, it is reasonable to inquire about the sexual history of your potential mate. It is just as reasonable to require, or at a minimum acquire, medical documentation of sexual status—infected or uninfected—before proceeding to the marriage altar. God's blessings make marriages spiritually clean, but only you can make them naturally so.

Summary Points:

- Sexually transmitted infections are prolific and widespread in the world.
- Christians can and do sometimes harbor sexually transmitted infections and spread them from one to another.
- It is very reasonable to test for sexually transmitted infections prior to marriage.

Discussion Questions:

- How would/should you begin the discussion of sexually transmitted infections with a potential mate? When should such discussions take place?
- What if your mate does not want to participate in discussions about and/or be tested for STIs?

- How can a person who has never copulated spread STIs?
- What *barriers* to STIs do you know?
- What is the church's role in dealing with the problem of STIs?
- What is the deadliest STI in this present world?

Is It Hard to Get It Up?

With advancing age, various forms of disease and injury, many Christian men find coital, sexual responsibilities problematic, and this difficulty can result in lack of sexual satisfaction on the part of the wife, and stress and lowered self-esteem on the part of the husband. Erectile dysfunction (ED) is frequently the basis of this sexual problem. Erectile dysfunction is the inability to sustain penile erection sufficient enough for penetrative sexual intercourse—copulation; men so affected have difficulty achieving erection and/or maintaining one during sexual intercourse.

It is estimated that more than 30 million men are affected by ED, but only 20 percent of that group seek help; this is mostly because men don't want to admit they have this problem, or want to talk about it. An individual experiencing ED should prayerfully and confidentially seek help to remedy this predicament. There are many professionals who can give counsel, direction, support, and therapy. A number of medical solutions to ED have been found.

Erectile dysfunction is not inevitable. Many seniors are capable of performing coitus and enjoy this form of sexual interplay for as long as they live. Deuteronomy 34:7 is a verse of hope and encouragement for all men; it tells that "Moses was an hundred and twenty years old when he died: his eye was not dim, nor his natural force abated." This verse, among other things, speaks to the natural virility and strength of Moses and reminds us that God can physically bless whomever he wants, however he wants, for as long as he wants.

What is inevitable with the aging of most men is the decreased production of testosterone. The decline of this sex hormone usually starts after age thirty. When men are in their sexual prime, a passing breeze can cause an erection. As men age, however, a lot more has to be stirring for them to achieve and maintain a suitable erection. Women should take particular note of this age-related erectile function and hormone decrease and realize they may need to increase their efforts to stimulate their man over time, rather than decrease these arousal tactics. So, women must work harder to start their spouses' sexual fire and then continue to stoke the coals while sexual intercourse is going on. Often aging men show reduced attention to copulation, not because they are truly uninterested, but because they have difficulty performing as in earlier years. They reduce their sexual encounters because of embarrassment and deflated egos and to not further disappoint their wives by being unable to complete the sex act.

Lowered testosterone also leads to muscle loss, increased abdominal girth, bone thinning, and reduced libido, among other things. Men and women can experience reduced interest in sex, but men seem to have libido problems less often than they have ED. In other words, men want to do it (copulate), but physically cannot. When a man does have reduced libido or sexual apathy, the causes can be varied.

Consider these words from Matthew 19:12: "For there are some eunuchs, which were so born from their mother's womb; and there are some eunuchs, which were made eunuchs of men: and there be eunuchs, which have made themselves eunuchs for the kingdom of heaven's sake." This scripture points out that a man's sexual indifference can have a physical/congenital cause ("from their mother's womb"), a man-made cause—surgery, injury, drugs ("made eunuchs of men"), or a spiritual cause ("for the kingdom of heaven's sake").

A man (such as in the case of Apostle Paul) may choose to abstain from sex because of his concentration on and dedication to the work of the Lord.

> For I would that all men were even as I myself [celibate]. But every man hath his proper gift of God, one after this manner, and another after that. I say therefore to the unmarried and widows, it is good for them if they abide even as I. But if they cannot contain, let them marry: for it is better to marry than to burn.
>
> 1 Corinthians 7:7–9

When either a man or a woman has problems with their libido, these matters should be discussed with their spouse and then taken to a professional who is facile, comfortable, and competent to deal with such issues. Never suffer in silence if your sexual life is out of kilter. God did not intend for this part of our existence to be a burden, but rather a blessing. When erectile dysfunction is caused by or added to the condition of lowered testosterone and libido, the circumstance can be challenging for a married couple still interested in coitus.

When a man has difficulty getting and maintaining an erection, it often has negative impact on his psyche leading to humiliation and guilt. He may over compensate during sexual encounters, or try too hard to will a sufficient erection leading to stress and anxiety. Stress and anxiety set an individual up for poor sexual performance, and the problem can become cyclic and difficult to solve.

A man's spouse can be extremely helpful at times of sexual impotence. A wife's attitude about ED and her actions toward her husband either help ease the guilt and pressure he is feeling or exacerbate the situation. A couple should prayerfully and openly discuss this condition (at a time when sexual intercourse is not in play) and together make plans to deal with it. The wife should give her husband loving reassurance and earnestly assist him to attain and maintain the erection he so much wants to have; this should be a time for caressing, stroking, and whatever other tactile and emotional stimulation is needed. It is estimated that 20 percent of all erectile dysfunction is due to psychogenic reasons. Counseling, therapy, and loving encouragement can help many men get over ED when it has a non-organic cause.

Without question, however, there are organic reasons for ED—diabetes, kidney disease, multiple sclerosis, Parkinsonism, spinal cord injury, pelvic surgery, prostatic disease, radiation, and especially atherosclerosis. Penetrative sexual intercourse requires a well-functioning nervous system, adequate testosterone level, good vascular blood flow, and healthy genitalia. There must be unimpeded, physiologic interplay between all these systems as well as sensory and psychogenic stimuli if coitus is to take place.

When blood vessels of the body are unhealthy, limiting the flow of blood, this phenomenon is not confined to just one area of the body (most of us are familiar with coronary artery blockage), but tends to be present in all organ systems, including the male reproductive system. Men who have diseased coronaries and/or diabetes, with compromised blood vessels, will likely have some degree of erectile dysfunction as well. When medicine side effects (antihypertensive, antihistamine, diuretic, etc.) are added to this organic disease scenario, ED can really wreak havoc on the sexual relationships of loving, committed, Christian couples.

Fortunately, we live in an age where numerous drugs, surgical remedies, and therapies are available to assist those who suffer from ED. Some of these drugs can be had by prescription only; others can be bought over the counter, through the mail, or via the Internet. Plus, diet, especially one rich in leafy green vegetables, has been shown to be beneficial in ED treatment.

There are many scams aimed at men with erectile dysfunction. Most unscrupulous remedies come with little or no evidence-based proof or research to back claims. Many also seek upfront payment (usually via credit card) and long term subscriptions for their products or treatments. Use caution when seeking remedies and consult your medical practitioner. Nothing in the Bible speaks against using such drugs or copulatory aids to ED, be they medicinal, surgical, or naturopathic. Any Christian man who is having a hard time copulating should avail himself of the help now available through modern medicine and continue to enjoy this precious sexual gift given by our God.

In addition, couples, remember to be creative. So often where there's a sexual will, there's a sexual way! Copulation is not the only path to sexual pleasure, satisfaction, or orgasm. Working together with your spouse, you may well find enjoyable alternatives and/or supplements to penile sexual intercourse and also receive the unexpected bonus of a more diverse sexual repertoire.

Summary Points:

- Men often experience erectile dysfunction as they age or as the result of disease or surgery.
- Erectile dysfunction should be discussed with your wife and professional help sought as needed.
- There are many aids to erectile dysfunction in today's society. Christian men should take advantage of these advances to deal with this ailment.

Discussion Questions:

- What is the female spouse's role in male erectile dysfunction?
- When erectile dysfunction is psychogenic in origin, what should be the solution?
- How can you distinguish psychogenic origin ED from organic or structural?
- How does arterial disease relate to erectile dysfunction; what's the mechanism at work?
- A man with erectile dysfunction is at risk for what other type diseases?
- If a man can get it up, what can a spouse do to help him keep it up?
- What do you think of ads for erectile dysfunction? Are they right on? Overdone?

Why Isn't She Interested?

Not too many years ago, women who showed less than enthusiastic interest in sexual intercourse—particularly coitus—were referred to as *frigid*. The word frigid (inhibited in the ability to express sexual excitement during sexual activity; without ardor or enthusiasm) carried a negative connotation. This label was usually placed on a woman by a man (doctor or otherwise) when a woman did not live up to the sexual expectations of a man. It shouldn't take a genius to see the flaw in this type labeling or diagnosing. In the male-dominated societies of the time, the practice of referring to women as frigid was somewhat self-serving and punitive.

The word *frigidity* is little used in enlightened, contemporary medicine. Women and men who have a flagging interest in sexual matters—especially coitus—are now thought to have a sexual disorder described as *hypoactive sexual desire, inhibited sexual desire,* or *sexual aversion/apathy*. It is unlikely that women affected by *inhib-*

ited sexual desire are happy in their circumstance. Such women usually don't want to have an aversion to sex, but do so because something has gone wrong with their sexual mechanism.

A healthy sexual mechanism requires a reasonably healthy mind, body, and spirit open to sexual intimacy. Any number of things can happen to cause insult to that sexual mechanism, such that it does not function as originally planned. What is important to understand in these unfortunate situations is that decreased interest in sex can have multifactorial causes, and not be because a woman *just doesn't like it* (sex)!

In preceding chapters, you have read the basic premise that God created sex and sexual desire to assure procreation, but also for pleasure and intimate bonding. We are programmed to achieve pleasure from sexual intercourse, and few of us turn our noses up at the concept of sexual pleasure, stimulation, and/or orgasm. It is not God's will that our sexual appetites be inordinately blunted for long periods of time. Most people will have times when they simply are not interested in engaging in sexual interplay; this can be for reasons of illness, exhaustion, anger, surroundings, geographical separation, etc.

For example, in Genesis 20:6, it was God who dulled the sex drive of Abimilech so he would not take Abraham's wife, Sarah, to bed. Abraham, after coming to the kingdom of Gerar, introduced his wife Sarah as his sister. Abraham was afraid that the king of Gerar, Abimilech, would kill him because he was Sarah's husband and then take Sarah as a wife or concubine—all because of her beauty. Convinced Sarah was Abraham's sister, and therefore available, Abimilech did take her back to his dwelling and would have had sex with her, but God made Abimilech "a dead man for the woman" (verse three). God squashed Abimilech's libido to honor his covenant with Abraham, saying to the king, "I also withheld thee from sinning against me: therefore suffered I thee not to touch her" (verse six).

As another example, think again of the story of Joseph in Genesis chapter thirty-nine. Potiphar's wife very much wanted Joseph to have sex with her and had arranged for privacy and convenience so that the intercourse could take place. Joseph instead forthrightly declined her offer. In verse nine of this chapter, he says to Potiphar's wife: "There is none greater in this house than I; neither hath he [Potiphar] kept back anything from me but thee, because thou art his wife: how then can I do this great wickedness, and sin against God?" Joseph deliberately curbed his sexual appetite so that he would not sin against God. In this matter, he is the poster boy for sexual integrity.

The final example of a blunted sex drive features Amnon, whose illicit sexual desire for his half-sister Tamar was totally erased after he had forced himself on her, scripture explains:

> But, being stronger than she, forced her, and lay with her. Then Amnon hated her exceedingly; so that the hatred wherewith he hated her was greater than the love wherewith he had loved her. And Amnon said unto her, Arise, be gone.
>
> 2 Samuel 13: 14–15

The point behind these three examples is that there are a number of reasons why an individual might not be interested in sex, an act of God—such as what happened with Abimilech (some physical condition over which the person has no control), an act of conscience (as in Joseph's instance), or guilt and self-hate (as with Amnon). These are but a few reasons sexual aversion/apathy may be present.

When a lack of sexual interest is the rule and not the exception, *hypoactive sexual desire* must be considered as a possible diagnosis. Male erectile dysfunction was discussed in an earlier chapter. Let's now look at how sexual dysfunction might impact women.

Having sexual desire for your husband is normal, and wanting to demonstrate that desire emotionally and physically is a normal expression. When the desire is not present (except for brief periods) something has gone very wrong; this something can have physical, emotional, or environmental causes, among others.

Just as in a man, testosterone is key for a woman's sex drive; there must be a good balance of this hormone along with estrogen. In the absence of adequate testosterone, a woman's libido wanes. Lowered testosterone can be the byproduct of surgery, especially total hysterectomy or oophorectomy, since the ovaries are responsible for testosterone production. Menopause and accompanying hormonal changes can have a dulling affect on a woman's sexual drive. Postmenopausal estrogen loss can lead to vaginal changes—thinning and drying of mucosal tissue, so much so that coitus is painful and physically irritating. Sometimes the dieting and exercise habits of a woman can lead to hormonal changes that lead to decreased libido.

We must never forget the emotional make up of a woman and the critical part psychological state plays in a woman's receptivity to sexual intercourse. For generations, Christian women were expected to be discreet and not display their sexual personalities. Now we have flipped the script and want them to let it all hang out (their sexual identities) in the bedroom, and many women have difficulty making the adjustment in sexual temperament. Husbands must be understanding of this historical inconsistency and be gentle with their sexual requests when necessary.

Don't underestimate the impact a woman's past sexual experiences has on her current sexual performance. It is estimated that at least one-third of all adult women have been sexually assaulted at some level at some time in their lives. There may be depression from past abusive experiences and anxiety about present ones. As a result of earlier sexual traumas, many women will have hang-ups about sexual expression and will be uncertain about proper ways to indicate their sexual preferences and wishes. When women have been abused and dominated by men, often sexual repression and/or hesitancy is the only control these women have. While this is not a healthy situation, it certainly should be considered when looking for causes of *sexual aversion*.

As mentioned in another chapter, men (generally speaking) are more genital-oriented and see copulation as a way of expressing love. Whereas women (generally speaking) process love cues on many more intangible levels than their genitals, with copulation often being a result of that process.

If a husband has not captured the mind of his wife, it is unlikely he will ever truly possess her body. With this in mind, it is easy to see how excess stress and the overall unhealthy status of a marriage relationship can put a damper on sexual interplay. Husbands, look at the overall quality of your marriage relationship when the sex isn't what you desire! Often the amount and quality of the sex is a measure of the healthiness of the relationship.

Environmental causes that deter a robust sex life come in many forms for a woman. Simple things like relatives or children in a nearby room, bills that haven't been paid, or loved ones who are ill can seriously curtail the sexual desire of a woman. While women can be as adventurous and spontaneous as any man, most seek a secure, private environment to express their sexuality. Self-image is important also. A husband shouldn't spend most of the day running his wife down for one reason or another and then expect her to be a sexual dynamo when he's ready for bed. How a woman feels about herself translates quite faithfully into how she expresses her sexual self in the marriage bed.

Finally, before blaming your wife, check yourself, husbands. Have you been kind to your wife? Have you made the surroundings and mood conducive for sex? Is your hygiene adequate? Have you arranged for the right aromas? Are you clean-shaven (unless she likes it the other way around)? Is your breath all that it should be? Get my drift?

A healthy sex drive for both spouses is what God intended. In marriage, sex has a tendency to either bond us closer to one another or cause barriers to be put up that make for a very unpleasant existence together. When you want to know, "Why isn't she interested?" first ask your wife. Ask in a frank, loving, and unintimidating way, then, if necessary, seek professional help. Utilizing Godly advisors, sex therapists, physicians, allopath, homeopath, naturopath, and others skilled in matters of inhibited sexual drive, couples can usually find answers that will restore joy and pleasure to the marriage bed.

Summary Points:

- If a woman has inhibited sexual desire there is usually an environmental, psychological or physical cause.
- Christians with inhibited sexual desire should communicate honestly with their spouse and seek professional counsel where needed.
- Help is available for sexual apathy; seek it out. Pray about your situation and don't suffer in silence.

Discussion Questions:

- Why do you think Amnon no longer wanted Tamar after having sex with her? (2 Samuel 13)
- Is it true that men just have a stronger sex drive than women?

- Are some people born with a decreased interest in sex? What about an increased interest? Explain.
- Past abuse can affect current sexual interest and performance. How should a married couple deal with past abuse against one or both of the partners?
- What is the main thing a woman with inhibited sexual desire needs from her husband?

What About Polygamy?

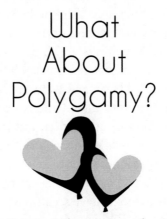

There are numerous polygamous cultures around the globe, but in the United States, the practice is illegal and very controversial. Polygamy is the practice or condition of having more than one spouse at a time. Most recently, a polygamous group located in Texas was much in the news because of this lifestyle and the children born of these sexual unions. That group's beliefs were pitted against the power of the U.S. government to challenge or regulate such behavior.

The religious community does not agree on whether the Bible sanctions or condemns polygamy, and for the time being, most U.S. polygamists are fairly surreptitious in their behavior, preferring to avoid public scrutiny of the lifestyle or discussions of this topic unless pushed.

The main arguments for polygamy come from Bible scriptures that describe polygamous relationships. The following are a few examples: "And David took him more concubines and wives out of Jerusalem, after he

was come from Hebron: and there were yet sons and daughters born to David" (2 Samuel 5:13).

Concerning Solomon: "And he had seven hundred wives, princesses, and three hundred concubines: and his wives turned away his heart" (1 Kings 11:3).

It is well known that the patriarch Abraham had three wives, Sarah, Hagar, and Keturah, as well as concubines: "But unto the sons of the concubines, which Abraham had, Abraham gave gifts, and sent them away from Isaac his son, while he yet lived, eastward, unto the east country" (Genesis 25:6).

Admittedly, these type unions are rife throughout the Bible. Proponents believe scriptural descriptions of plural marriages by Bible patriarchs give tacit consent for present day polygynous and polyandrous unions. Polygynous (many wives) unions far outnumber polyandrous (many husbands) ones; polygamy is a term used to refer to both type associations.

The main arguments against the practice of polygamy stem from Bible verses that specify or infer one husband, one wife relationships. An example is 1 Corinthians 7:2: "Nevertheless to avoid fornication, let every man have his own wife, and let every woman have her own husband."

The following paragraphs will not settle the polygamy matter, but will offer an opinion after a very brief review of the topic.

In times past, polygamy was most often the privilege of kings and patriarchs. Also, it was an off-shoot of the pastoral lifestyle and of a circumstance where humans lived in isolated clusters. Members of such communities frequently chose their mates based on availability, and those available mates were many times first, second, and third degree relatives. Because these societies were most often patriarchal, males usually got to choose and chose more than one mate at a time out of custom, paternalism, necessity, or greed. In circumstances where males outnumbered females, women sometimes had the privilege of choosing more than one male at a time. Nonetheless, most arguments about polygamy center on polygyny.

Some say polygamy was a consequence of warring nations and the subsequent decimation of the male population in given areas. When one added to this equation the persistence of male-dominated societies, group mores steered single women toward relationships where they would be protected by the male, even if other women were members of the same household.

Biblical examples of polygamy are thought to stem from some or all of the above-mentioned reasons. And while the Old Testament has numerous examples of polygamous relationships, the New Testament does not, but rather emphasizes monogamy. Many contemporary Christians speak against polygamy for this reason alone, asserting that the Old Testament ways are passé and the New Testament is a better guide of how believers should live their lives today. There is no compelling reason for polygamy as a lifestyle in modern society, except as a conscious choice based on beliefs.

This chapter is not meant to be a polemic on polygamy. However, one of the main verses used by both sides to put forth their arguments about polygamy is Genesis 2:24—"Therefore shall a man leave his father and his mother, and shall cleave unto his wife: and they shall be one flesh."

The polygamist will point out that the verse does not say a man can't *be one* with more than one woman. The monogamist will emphasize two people becoming *one flesh*, and the implication that one flesh equals one union only between two people and not many unions. If you've been around church people for any length of time, you're well aware of how two people can take a single scripture and spin it many different ways. These two opposing viewpoints about polygamy have been around for centuries, and there's no great likelihood the argument will soon be mutually settled. Add the fact that many isolated, non-modern, non-westernized cultures still practice polygamy unabashedly, and this is a topic that will confound religious discussions for years to come.

No side-by-side comparison of alleged pro and con scriptures is done here, but there are probably as many Bible verses that could be used to argue for polygamy as there are verses that could be used to refute the practice. The several polygamous relationships documented in Scripture can be countered by the prominent monogamous ones. When the Bible does not explicitly give guidance about a particular custom through some single passage, then we must consider the preponderance of guidance that is given.

Therefore, polygamy, while present in the Bible, is a custom of the past. It has little place in today's Christian society, or especially in these United States where it is illegal. Christians are certainly admonished to follow the laws of the land when those laws do not clearly and directly conflict with the laws of God—"Let every soul be subject unto the higher powers. For there is no power but of God: the powers that be are ordained of God" (Romans 13:1).

Polygamy runs smack up against God's wish that marriage be a sacred, permanent contract between one man and one woman. Extending that contract to others simultaneously erodes and often destroys the one-on-one bond God intended for a married couple. Polygamy also opens the door to too many other characterizations of marriage, and the slippery slope of following societies' ever-changing whims about the subject. An insightful person once wrote, "When marriage becomes anything, it becomes nothing." I agree with this principle and take my stand with the legions who speak against polygamy. May God bless and guide you as you set your course and stake out your position on this subject.

Summary Points:

- Polygamy is alive and thriving in clusters of modern society and is a controversial practice among Christians.
- Polygamy is against the law in the United States.
- Polygamy, while well-documented in the Bible, is a lifestyle from our past and not the proper path for Christians of today.

Discussion Questions:

- Where do you stand on the issue of polygamy?
- What are the advantages and disadvantages of a polygamous relationship?
- Give an example of a polyandrous culture—historical or otherwise. What were the supposed virtues of this lifestyle?
- Are most polygamous relationships in the United States concentrated in a certain region?

Is There Any Exception for Contraception?

Contraception is a topic related to all the sexual practices mentioned in this book. Contraceptives and their use are equally as controversial as polygamous relationships, and the Christian community does not agree on this subject either. Opinion is as divided, unfortunately, as the numerous denominations are divided, and even fluctuates within discreet religious groups. Contraception is the deliberate prevention of conception or implantation by various drugs, techniques, or devices.

At one end of the contraceptive argument is the belief that copulation is first and foremost a procreative act and anything done to suppress procreative ability is sin. At the other end of the contraception spectrum is a focus on the unitive aspects of copulation, and the belief that sex should be enjoyed free of the possibility of procreation, if two people so choose. These two divergent opinions have been around for generations and no lessening of the argument looms on the horizon.

A large, time-tested, international body of religious believers forthrightly teaches that any form of contraception is anti-Christian and cites numerous theological, supporting opinions. The writers and scriptures cited, however, are only inferential, and the theological opinions are one-sided at best. Even within this thriving group, there are dissident attitudes and practices regarding contraception.

There are few Bible scriptures that refer directly to contraception. There are some scriptures where the idea of contraception is described. Onanism was discussed earlier in this book. The act of coitus interruptus described in the story of Onan is a form of birth control. Also, Bible writings refer often to surgical eunuchs—ostensibly one of the most radical forms of birth control. Matthew 19:12 reads (in part): "There are some eunuchs, which were made eunuchs of men," which is to say, either deliberately or accidentally, an individual was castrated. At one point in the Bible, Old Testament, eunuchs were barred from the congregation; they were barred because they could not produce sperm and subsequently impregnate a woman. Those against birth control make great use of this scripture as a definite condemnation of contraception practice: "He that is wounded in the stones, or hath his privy member cut off, shall not enter into the congregation of the Lord" (Deuteronomy 23:1).

This scripture is not a condemnation of birth control; it most likely speaks against the practice of self-mutilation and/or socially ostracizes those men who have intentionally or unintentionally been castrated. These words were written at a time of widespread male societal dominance. Then, as now, the intact, fertile male anatomy was the preeminent model of masculinity; the ability to father children also was highly prized. The seat of a man's virility—his testicles and their ability to produce the male sex hormone (testosterone) and sperm—were highly regarded. So, since this model was thought to be perfect; it was the idea of perfection that was acceptable and desirable for the congregation— only the best for the Lord.

Notice verse two: "A bastard shall not enter into the congregation of the Lord; even to his tenth generation." Do any of the readers of this book believe the bastard proscription should be true today, as well? Neither is the prohibition against a castrated male. In this day and age, one must surely question whether being a bastard or being castrated are sins, but even if they were, God's grace would be sufficient for all that and more.

In today's society, some men are chemically or surgically castrated for therapeutic reasons. We would hardly bar these men and ones who have been accidentally castrated from participating in worship within our churches. To use this scripture and Leviticus 21:20 to rail against contraception is to misconstrue the meaning of those scriptures and fail to consider their context. The Leviticus chapter twenty-one scripture also speaks of having your *stones broken* as being a blemish and bars the blemished—the *blind ... lame ... flat nose ... broken-footed* (and several others)—from the congregation.

On closer examination of this scripture, however, we find that such individuals were not barred from the congregation as a whole, but from offering "the bread of His God" (verse seventeen) within the congregation.

When read accurately, these proscriptions are aimed at Aaron and his specific Levitical descendents (a select group), not at all people who entered the congregation. God's church is not a place where the blemished or the infirm are to be excluded, but a place where they are to be welcomed. Surely all Christians agree on this point.

The Bible specifically commands Christians to "be fruitful, and multiply and replenish the earth" (Genesis 1:28). Few Christians argue over the proliferative meaning of this verse, or over the belief that children are a blessing from the Lord. However, excluding situations of unwanted infertility and those where a couple is actively trying to *have children*, few Christians are hoping to become pregnant every time they copulate.

Most Christians interpret Genesis 1:28 to mean procreate up to a point, but at some juncture, give the decision about whether to become pregnant and when to me. Those who buy into this interpretation are usually using some means, however simple, to prevent the unplanned pregnancy. The argument, therefore, comes over whether married couples have the right to plan parenthood and whether contraceptives can be used to carry out those plans.

Absent any specific biblical directive, decisions about whether to use birth control become a matter of individual conscience. And while spousal partners should discuss this matter both before and during marriage, most contraception decisions are easily more personal to the female spouse than to the male. This is true because contraceptives directed at women and the female physiology, are much more prolific than those directed at the male. In those instances, where the contraceptive modality affects the male physiology predominantly, then of course the decision is more personally his.

So, God doesn't make an exception for contraception because there was never a rule against it. As regards the definition given at the outset of this chapter, God does speak against birth control modalities that prevent *implantation*. Implantation occurs after an egg has been fertilized and life has begun. The rule that was given to Christians unequivocally was: "Thou shalt not kill" (Exodus 20:13). And to that end, Christians who practice birth control should take great pains to choose a method that is not abortifacient. An abortifacient is a drug, substance, or devise used to cause abortion. There is nothing in the Bible that should prevent you from having some say about the timing, frequency, and nature of your pregnancy, but everything about the Bible speaks to you being ardently in favor of human life and doing nothing to harm an unborn child, regardless of its stage of development.

Summary Points:

- The use of contraceptives is a highly controversial practice among Christians and the church body is effectively polarized around this issue.
- It is acceptable to use various methods to prevent unwanted pregnancies.
- The use of contraceptives should be discussed and agreed upon with your spouse.

- Whatever methods are chosen, abortifacients should never be used.
- Give your thoughts on how long you think people have been practicing birth control.

Discussion Questions:

- What percentages of Christians practice no form of birth control at all?
- How effective is *coitus interruptus* and calendar-based methods in preventing unwanted pregnancy?
- What's the difference between a contraceptive and an abortifacient?
- If Christians are to "be fruitful and multiply," what if a married couple chooses not to have children? Is that choice a sin?

Epilogue

The more I think about it, the more I'm convinced my wife's question to me should not have been "Can we do that?" but "Is it right for us to do that?" We live in a world that is making enormous strides in science, medicine, and other technologies. Unfortunately, it is also a world where no holds barred sexuality is fast becoming the norm. The truth is, we *can* do a number of things that were only dreamed about in years past—cloning, genetic engineering, embryonic stem cell research and therapy, same-sex marriage, sex-change surgery (to name only a few)—but *should we* do them is the more legitimate question. Are the mores of today's society ethical, moral, or biblical?

The world makes little attempt to hide its sexual appetites or exploits, and the sex lives of celebrities is daily fodder for the visual and print media. These overtly sexual images and words are constantly bombarding our eyes, entering our minds and changing our hearts. The kind of explicit sex one can access through

 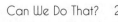

the Internet, via the mail, and on special TV channels brings millions face to face with sexual intercourse in all its forms, some of them more base than others—literally sex on parade. Prime time TV networks are not far behind, either, in terms of the hedonism they serve up on a daily basis. Television programming guidelines seem to be the more titillating, the better! Propriety is no longer valued and the boundaries of decency are being pushed far afield.

Most of the sex scenes we are shown through the media are not fit for general public viewing; they certainly should not be shown to impressionable children and should not be the core of a Christian's entertainment. It is not spiritually uplifting for godly individuals to have such steady exposure to someone else's sex play, especially when most all the acts shown are the product of illicit, immoral relationships.

Watching erotica over and over again desensitizes the minds of many Christians and causes them to think such behavior is normal and acceptable. Christians must steadfastly question and challenge the world's sexual norms and ultimately base their amorous actions on biblical principles instead.

In this world, Christians will have to choose daily whether they will follow godly principles and practices, and they will have to be very deliberate about the choice. For the sake of our spiritual sanity and sanctity, sometimes we will have to turn off, look away, or run away from the sexual sins that are so prevalent in today's world. It is not easy to avoid the sensual messages and imagery that comes at us from so many directions. For this reason, we must intentionally reject these overly erotic displays and shield our children from their influence.

Don't kid yourself; it is easy to succumb to blatantly sexual messages and images, thereby compromising our moral beliefs and standards. Sex is powerfully attractive and often only a key stroke or button's click away. Some Christians rationalize exposing themselves and their children to society's sexual norms, believing that the exposure informs their lives and helps them understand the world around them. Christians, however, are called upon to live in this world but not take on its values.

John 17:15 explains, using Jesus' words: "I have given them thy word; and the world hath hated them, because they are not of the world, even as I am not of the world. I pray not that thou shouldest take them out of the world, but that thou shouldest keep them from the evil."

Make no mistake about it, in this world, those who stand firm for Jesus and for living a committed, biblically principled life will be in the minority, will not be popular, and most likely will be ridiculed for doing so. But there's something very familiar about being in such a position in society; it is pretty much a litmus test for whether we are living our lives in accordance with God's plan. In Matthew 5:10–11, Jesus taught: "Blessed are they which are persecuted for righteousness' sake for theirs is the kingdom of heaven. Blessed are ye when men shall revile you, and persecute you, and shall say all manner of evil against you falsely, for my sake."

Committed Christians must be prepared to be derided by the world for taking a stand against sexual immorality, but "great is your reward" (verse twelve), the scripture tells. This scripture implies there is great spiritual reward both now and later for standing firm on God's principles and precepts.

Civilization's rules will change much faster than they did over the past three to four generations, and Christians will be confronted as never before about their belief system. We must be prepared to stand firm and to explain our stand based on the principles intoned in God's Holy Word. It is not that we will see new sins, but the sins we see will come packaged in new, colorful ways. Dressed in rationalizations and sanctioned by high-profile individuals, these sins will be more difficult to recognize and renounce.

The sexually depraved populations of this world are increasing in number much faster than the sexually discreet, and our society encourages the trend. The world prizes deliberate sensuality far more than dedicated sanctification, and the church has lost the battle for the sexual spirit. The fact that we have lost this battle does not mean we should stop fighting. Christians ultimately will win the war against sin, and our mission (with the help of the Lord) should be to win back the hearts and minds of the world's captives. God's amazing grace can save any soul from any sin. Once they are in the fold, we should indoctrinate them in the ways of the Master. As we are teaching Christians about salvation, sanctification, and spirituality, we must also teach them about Godly sexual behavior. If we don't teach them the ways of the Lord, the void will most certainly be filled with the ways of the world—a malevolent moral code.

Many of the people we seek to lead to Christ will have already indulged in sexual intercourse earlier and on a number of levels. Many will be physically and emotionally scarred from their forays into this world of carnality. Though willing to accept the Master and the new life he has for them, these converts will be broken and guilt-ridden, believing they cannot leave behind the stain of their past deeds.

We must love these individuals and assure them that the grace of God is equal to and sufficient for all situations. We must reason with them and remind them of the words of Isaiah 1:18: "Though your sins be as scarlet, they shall be as white as snow; though they be red like crimson, they shall be as wool." God's willingness and power to forgive is far greater than a person's propensity to sin; his grace is sufficient! Once these converts have seen and recognized the face of Jesus, the next faces they see, ours, should be filled with compassion and acceptance. I cannot overemphasize the need for us to lead with love, even when we disagree with another's chosen lifestyle or belief system. Never forget that all of us have sinned, none of us are perfect, and it is only the grace and the power of the Holy Spirit that keeps us walking the godly way.

We are God's remnant. We will be challenged in the boardrooms where we work, the classrooms where we teach and learn, the streets we walk on a daily basis, and the bedrooms where we live and love. The very identity and relevance of the church will be called into question around sexual issues, and we must be prepared to give consistent, cogent, scripturally-based answers. The questions will come up again and again, "Can we

do this? Is it right for us to do that? What does the Bible have to say on these matters?"

How will we handle the imminent threat to marriage as an institution blessed by God and sacred between a man and a woman? The world's forces have arrayed themselves in opposition to this God-sanctioned, time-honored relationship, and their influence is growing–sweeping across our nation and world. Holy Scripture teaches: "For we wrestle not against flesh and blood, but against principalities, against powers, against the rulers of the darkness of this world, against spiritual wickedness in high places" (Ephesians 6:12). We must be prepared to speak up and take a forthright, biblically-based stand on matters of marriage and sexual conduct, but our ultimate weapons for fighting such influences must be more fasting and prayer than fact sheets and legal opposition. It is prayer that is "mighty through God to the pulling down of strong holds" (2 Corinthians 10:4). Let's be candid, though, the *handwriting on the wall* says that the world will win this battle too and will sinfully redefine the marriage union; if not this year, then soon. Just remember that the world's definitions must not determine the conduct of God's people.

How will we handle the glorification of children born outside of marriage and the deification of celebrities who flaunt licentious lifestyles? What will we say to our children who are taught by society that premarital sex is to be expected and planned for rather than a situation to avoid? Our culture has successfully shifted the standard from stable marriages and nuclear families to ever-transient relationships with *baby-daddies* and *baby-mommas*. The Christian who confronts such immoral unions is labeled by its practitioners as intolerant and abusive. Advocates of this new morality are convinced that they are right and that Christians are locked in some ill-informed, antiquated time warp.

Christians are not meant to be intolerant, but to deliver the ultimate form of tolerance—love for all, regardless of who they are, or what they may happen to believe. We must love people, but we must not love everything and anything people do, especially when their actions run smack up against the Word of God. One place where Christians are *peculiar* is in their belief that there is a criterion for conduct, and that the Bible is unequivocally that standard!

> There is a generation that curseth their father and doth not bless their mother. There is a generation that are pure in their own eyes, and yet is not washed from their filthiness. There is a generation, O how lofty are their eyes! And their eyelids are lifted up.
>
> Proverbs 30:11–13

What Christians must do is be as driven as the world—even more so, but driven by the Holy Spirit to stand firm for the Lord and the time-honored principles he has given us through his Word. Ours will not be an easy task, and at times it will be thankless, but we are called to be the salt (to help preserve the good) and light (to illuminate the way to God) for this world. We must not falter in this task; we must not be discouraged. Like Timothy, we must declare:

> For I know whom I have believed, and am persuaded that he is able to keep that which I have committed

unto him against that day. Hold fast the form of sound words, which thou has heard of me, in faith and love which is in Christ Jesus. That good thing which was committed unto thee keep by the Holy Ghost which dwelleth in us.

2 Timothy 1:12–14

Our determination must be to keep *that good thing*, which is God's instruction to us from the Bible. We must follow the rules and precepts of God as he has laid them out in his Word and as they relate to the time in which we live. Next, we must teach true and relevant precepts regarding Christian sexuality, and then spread that teaching as far as God will permit.

Won't you pray for me and work with me as I press this ministry for sexual clarity and genuineness within the church body? Will you help me spread the word? Will you tell someone about these and related sexual matters? Together, can we do that?

"As for me and my house,
we will serve the Lord"

Joshua 24:15

W.G. Robinson-McNeese, M.D.

Reverend Dr. McNeese is available to speak
about any and all topics within this book.
Contact him at Pastormd926@aol.com.

⊖|LIVE

---

listen|imagine|view|experience

AUDIO BOOK DOWNLOAD INCLUDED WITH THIS BOOK!

In your hands you hold a complete digital entertainment package. In addition to the paper version, you receive a free download of the audio version of this book. Simply use the code listed below when visiting our website. Once downloaded to your computer, you can listen to the book through your computer's speakers, burn it to an audio CD or save the file to your portable music device (such as Apple's popular iPod) and listen on the go!

How to get your free audio book digital download:

1. Visit www.tatepublishing.com and click on the e|LIVE logo on the home page.
2. Enter the following coupon code:
   a0fd-827a-fb50-fb3d-b627-762a-6ae4-2e11
3. Download the audio book from your e|LIVE digital locker and begin enjoying your new digital entertainment package today!